PATHWAYS T

AVUL PAKIR JAINULABDEEN ABDUL KALAM was the eleventh President of India, from 2002 to 2007. He was a recipient of the Padma Bhushan, the Padma Vibhushan and the nation's highest civilian award, the Bharat Ratna.

Born in 1931 in Rameswaram in Tamil Nadu, Dr Kalam studied aeronautical engineering at the Madras Institute of Technology. He played a key role in the development of India's first satellite launch vehicle, the SLV-3; in the building and operationalization of India's strategic missile systems; and in the 1998 nuclear tests.

As an elder statesman, he was in the public eye for his role in offering counsel, reaching out to people and building bridges across religious and social divides. Dr Kalam's focus was ever on transforming India into a developed nation by 2020 and to this end he continued to travel across the country for his teaching assignments at IITs and IIMs, to address conferences and to meet students and people from all walks of life.

He passed away at one such lecture he had gone to deliver at Shillong, Meghalaya, on 27 July 2015. His message and influence continue to resonate with people across the country and in all walks of life.

PATHWAYS TO GREATNESS

Coming Together for Change

A.P.J. ABDUL KALAM

HarperCollins *Publishers* India

First published in India in 2017 by
HarperCollins *Publishers* India

Copyright © A.P.J. Abdul Kalam 2017

P-ISBN: 978-93-5264-383-7
E-ISBN: 978-93-5264-384-4

2 4 6 8 10 9 7 5 3 1

A.P.J. Abdul Kalam asserts the moral right to be identified
as the author of this work.

The views and opinions expressed in this book
are the author's own and the facts are as reported by him,
and the publishers are not in any way liable for the same.

HarperCollins *Publishers*
A-75, Sector 57, Noida, Uttar Pradesh 201301, India
1 London Bridge Street, London, SE1 9GF, United Kingdom
Hazelton Lanes, 55 Avenue Road, Suite 2900, Toronto, Ontario M5R 3L2
and 1995 Markham Road, Scarborough, Ontario M1B 5M8, Canada
25 Ryde Road, Pymble, Sydney, NSW 2073, Australia
195 Broadway, New York, NY 10007, USA

Typeset in 11.5/16 Calisto MT by
R. Ajith Kumar

Printed and bound at
Thomson Press (India) Ltd.

Dedicated to the memory of
Major General R. Swaminathan (Retd)

CONTENTS

Contents

SECTION III: FINAL THOUGHTS

A NOTE ON THE BOOK

The house at 10 Rajaji Marg which Dr Kalam occupied after completing his term as President in July 2007 suited his requirements perfectly. There was a large lawn in front and at the back, with a path running around it which he used for walking whenever he needed to get some exercise. There was a formal receiving room on the ground floor, with an adjoining office where two of his trusted secretaries, H. Sheridon and R.K. Prasad, sat. Turning right in the passageway, there was a long flight of stairs with a blue carpet which had become a little faded over the years with constant use. At the end of it, to the left, were his private quarters. In front of the staircase, behind a door that was always partly open, was another office, where sat Major General R. Swaminathan (Retd), who was his chief of staff at Rashtrapati Bhavan as well as here, and another secretary, D.R. Sharma.

It was in this office that a lot of his ideas incubated from 2007 to his death on 27 July 2015, almost exactly eight years after he demitted the office of President. It was for all practical purposes his ideas lab. His travel routine, intensive while he was President, had become even more strenuous after 2007. He was keynote speaker at an endless number of conferences; there was a stream of inaugurations and launches, including those of a few books; and his continuing programme of presentations to chief ministers on how their states could be put on the fast track to development. These gave detailed overviews of a state's strengths, resources and requirements and carried his stamp of research and optimism. And there were, too, his own books, a remarkable number of which have become fixtures on bestseller lists. His travels were varied, to say the least, and not always to the easiest of places to reach, involving long dusty rides in the official car.

The idea for *Pathways to Greatness* came up in conversations while he was President. He interacted with thousands of people as chief guest at numerous conferences and seminars. These included those held by professional bodies and institutions representing doctors, nurses, lawyers, educationists, scientists from various disciplines, engineers, and the police. He had formed the habit of having participants at these conclaves take an oath promising to uphold the values, principles and dignity of their profession.

I wondered if these could be given more lasting value in the form of a book. It could include anecdotes and stories of people who succeeded despite odds in upholding honesty and integrity, and be an informal reminder to people of the value of their profession and their own role. The context was, in part, our undoubted ability to execute difficult projects and tasks brilliantly but to falter on some of the simpler things, and to build things but slip up on the maintenance, for instance.

He was an inspired teacher but abhorred anything that was pompous or appeared to be didactic. His own way of offering a suggestion was invariably gentle, and he could express an opinion on a sensitive issue in a way that caused no offence. I had often noticed this while this project was still under discussion and we were putting together stories and source material for it, including several books that I passed on to him to help provide context. However, whenever I suggested using past glory as inspiration for the future, he would have none of it. The past was done with, the glory then the product of a different time and circumstances. The problems today were different and on a much larger scale. For instance, the population of India was now well over a billion. Thinking about past glory would not deliver solutions now. It was the future that excited him.

The premise of *Pathways to Greatness* was simple: laws, rules and values cannot be dictated from top down – they have to form part of our own value system. There can be laws against corruption, for instance, but no law can really catch all cases. Or, another example, how will any law ensure that a doctor provides good care to a patient if all he is interested in is making money off him through fees and tests that may not be necessary? It is eventually up to an individual to abide by his values, to follow his own code of conduct. The oaths would be a ready reference and reminder.

Economic development is one key strand in a nation's health and happiness. It helps provide education, health and financial security. However, nations, like individuals, also go through difficult times. What happens in those times and how a nation responds then is also a good yardstick of development. Would an emphasis on economic strength alone then be sufficient to sustain us? A truly sustainable path to progress would be one where a nation, as an individual, is able to withstand hardship too without losing discipline. One where an individual could also think of the general good and respect compatriots.

These were some of the ideas discussed in meetings off and on as work progressed. He had submitted a revised draft saying he had done his part. At our last meeting, on 11 July 2015, we decided to dedicate the book to Major General Swaminathan, who had been his close friend and aide for many years until his death in 2013. 'Then we must do it,' Dr Kalam said to me as I left. When I called on 27 July to fix an appointment on his return from Shillong, however, Mr Sharma, who had accompanied him there for his address at the Indian Institute of Management, told me he was unwell. The sad truth came out in TV bulletins later that evening.

There were several books that were done while *Pathways to Greatness* was under way. A few months after he submitted his revised manuscript, he gave me another, co-written with Srijan Pal Singh, *Advantage India*, which was published in October 2015. *Pathways to Greatness* actually precedes it but has taken longer as I was reviewing it with him when he passed away. It is a book that makes an important point. Our own view was that it should be circulated on a very wide scale, to people from all walks of life, from students to householders to leaders, who could draw from and add to it. One of Dr Kalam's favourite quotes was: Small aim is a crime. In *Pathways to Greatness*, he emphasizes it once again, raising the bar for us in a book, one can say, that is of enduring value. It would have delighted him no end to see this book make a difference.

Editor
February 2017

PREFACE

FRIENDS, WHAT YOU hold now in your hands is my thirty-fifth book – written either independently or with a co-author. Many of the ones I have written so far have been bestsellers. Two of them, *Ignited Minds* and *Wings of Fire*, have sold more than a million copies. But I often asked myself what the message was that I was trying to convey. So far I have written about how our nation can be developed economically, the missions for India's youth, and sometimes about the events in the life of our country. But I felt I had missed something very important.

The idea behind *Pathways to Greatness* is that economic progress alone does not make a nation great. What is most important is national character, born out of the value systems that exist in our families, what schools teach students, and the culture of the nation. Let me explain with an example. I was once on a flight from Bhubaneswar to New Delhi, and almost half of the passengers were foreign tourists. After some time I went to the washroom just as one of the foreigners came out. I noticed that the wash basin and the toilet were completely clean. I have not seen this habit of cleaning up after one has used the toilet in many of my countrymen. Such habits are products of national character.

I often think what is it that we as a nation require to evolve our national character. What do we need to make that last-mile journey to what all the plans, investments and projects are meant to lead up to – to create a nation that is on a sustainable path to progress? I have realized that progress and development are only one part of the picture. A nation, like an individual, has to learn to survive in tough times too, to maintain control, balance, a positive approach and the ability to work with others. The nations that have truly made it – the ones that have an evolved society, a deep-rooted culture, effective governance and law and order, an administration that everybody cooperates with, and families that impart lasting values to their children – have worked together as a people to reach that stage. Each citizen does his or her bit to help carry forward the values of the nation.

We live in a world that is changing rapidly. The change is led by technology, whose advancements are so rapid that those who fall behind are separated from the leaders not by decades but by centuries. Alongside technological change is the change happening in society because of urbanization. All around us people's aspirations are rising. They are looking for jobs but not all will have a bright future in a tough market. In a country like ours, an ancient culture alone may not be enough to hold the social fabric together. We need to proactively seek ways to provide a decent and comfortable life to our citizens, one where there is respect for the rich and the poor, the young and the old, the healthy and the sick.

India has made a great deal of progress in many areas. It is only a matter of time before it can be called economically developed. But is it sufficient? Not at all. Because in terms of the quality of life of our citizens, we have a long way to go. This book, then, is a manifesto for a better human life. Here I have tried to identify what makes a nation great, and also compared the standards of living of other nations with India's. As always, I have drawn on my travel within and outside the country. I have drawn on my interactions with a number of people from various strata of society. And here I offer my observations about how the life of every average Indian can be transformed into one of dignity, purpose and, above all, divinity.

I have evolved unique oaths for students, teachers, farmers, civil servants and medical professionals to ensure that this better human life becomes possible for all. I urge parents to read this book and pass on its message to their children. I request teachers to study it and discuss it with their students. I request political leaders to read it and spread the word in Parliament and to the people of India.

Pathways to Greatness has been in the making for many years. I hope that the lessons I have tried to offer here help our nation withstand the forces of change and lead the whole world on the pathways to greatness.

A.P.J. Abdul Kalam
March 2015

SECTION I
MUSINGS

ONE

WHAT MAKES A NATION GREAT?

BEFORE WE LOOK at what makes a nation great, I would like to talk about the advances made in the research on human evolution. Traditionally, there have been two distinct approaches to understanding this. First is the archaeological evidence. The lessons that we have learnt from Mohenjo-daro and Harappa and many similar excavations the world over have been crucial. They have made many a civilization's way of living, culture and origins evident.

The second and more recent approach is propelled by advances in our understanding of the human genome. While the major part of the genome sequence is common between human beings, the small portions that do differ lead to the diversity that we find in the evolution of humans. Professor Phillip Tobias (1925–2012) of South Africa was a pioneer in the fields of genetics and palaeoanthropology and helped further our understanding of evolution over millions of years. His work opened new vistas of research for scientists the world over.

In April 2005, the National Geographic Society (NGS), International Business Machines (IBM) and the Waitt Foundation (an American organization that strives to protect and restore ocean health) launched the Genographic Project, a genetic anthropological study that aims to map historical human migration patterns by collecting and analysing DNA samples from hundreds of thousands of people across five continents. Professor R.M. Pitchappan of the Madurai Kamaraj University is also working on this project, and my discussions with him have been thought-provoking.

Perhaps, some day in the future, the answer to the question 'What makes a nation great?' will be found in the human gene. For now, suffice it to say that the citizens of a nation are greater than the nation itself. It is they – their creative leadership, their pride of belonging to the nation and their vision – who in turn make the nation they live in great.

MAHATMA GANDHI, DR NELSON MANDELA AND HIS SOUTH AFRICA

I had a unique experience a few years ago that revealed to me how a single leader can inspire a large population. I happened to meet in Delhi the granddaughter of Mahatma Gandhi, Mrs Sumitra Gandhi Kulkarni. She narrated to me an anecdote about her grandfather which she had witnessed herself.

Gandhiji used to hold prayer meetings at a fixed time every evening. After the prayers, there would be a round of collection of donations for Harijan welfare, and the amount would be counted by his support staff. He would be informed of the amount before his dinner. The next day, a bank official would come to take the money. One day, the official reported that there was a discrepancy of a few paise between the money given to him and the amount collected. It was a small difference, but Gandhiji insisted that it was a donation for the poor and every paisa had to be accounted for. Such was the path of righteousness that Gandhiji trod as he led his nation and fellow countrymen on the path to greatness. All of us must follow his example and practise righteousness in all our thoughts and actions.

Here I would like to recall my journey of 16 September 2004 in the first-class compartment of a vintage South African train of the early twentieth century. As the train chugged from one station to another, Gandhiji's struggle against the injustices he had witnessed in that nation played on my mind. When I alighted at Pietermaritzburg, the station where he was evicted from the first-class compartment because of his skin colour, I saw a plaque commemorating him:

In the vicinity of this plaque
M.K. GANDHI was evicted
from a first-class
compartment on the night of
7 June 1893.

This incident changed
the course of his life.
He took up the fight
against racial oppression.
His active non-violence
started from that date.

As I stood there, my thoughts went back to two of my experiences in South Africa. One was in Robben Island, where Dr Nelson Mandela had been kept imprisoned for twenty-seven years in a very small cell. The other was at Dr Mandela's house.

Cape Town is famous for its Table Mountain. It has three peaks – Table Peak, Devil Peak and Fake Peak. It was a beautiful sight to behold between the peaks throughout the day as white and grey clouds embraced the summits alternately. Table Mountain is very close to the coast. From there I flew in a helicopter to Robben Island in ten minutes. When we reached there, except for the roaring of the sea, the whole island was silent. This was the place where the freedom of individuals was kept in shackles.

What surprised me was the size of the cell where Dr Mandela was kept. It was too tiny for a man of six feet to stay and sleep in for twenty-seven years. For a few hours every day he would be taken for quarrying in the nearby mountain in the bright sun. This was the time when his eyesight was damaged. In spite of his body being tortured, his spirit remained indomitable. He worked on a manuscript in tiny letters after the jail wardens went to sleep – what eventually became his famous book, *Long Walk to Freedom*.

It was a great event for me to meet him in his house in Johannesburg. What a moving reception the man gave at the age of eighty-six, all smiles. As I was leaving, he came to the portico to see me off. He discarded his walking stick and I became his support. I asked him, 'Dr Mandela, can you please tell me about the pioneers of the anti-apartheid movement in South Africa?'

He responded spontaneously, 'Of course. One of the great pioneers of South Africa's freedom movement was M.K. Gandhi. India gave us M.K. Gandhi and we gave you back Mahatma Gandhi after two decades.' That has indeed been India's tradition: to enrich whichever nation we go to, not only in financial terms but with knowledge, sweat and, above all, honour and dignity.

Dr Mandela, when he became the President of South Africa, gave the people who had ill treated him and kept him in jail for twenty-seven years the freedom to move about and to live in South Africa as equal citizens. Dear friends, an important lesson that we learn from this great personality was beautifully captured in one of the couplets of the Thirukkural written 2,200 years ago by the poet–saint Thiruvalluvar:

இன்னா செய்தாரை ஒறுத்தல் அவர்நாண

நன்னயம் செய்து விடல்

It means that the best response to those who do ill to you is to return good to them. Two political leaders, Mahatma Gandhi and Dr Nelson Mandela, indeed transformed India and South Africa respectively into independent, democratic nations with more than one-sixth of the world population. Their leadership paved the way for many nations to fight for freedom.

EUROPE

Let us now look at Europe and what lessons in greatness we can draw from it.

The European civilization has a unique place in human history. Its people explored this planet and are credited with groundbreaking ideas and developments in art, literature, music and science. But the continent was also a theatre of conflicts between nations for hundreds of years, including the two world wars of the previous century.

Despite this backdrop, Europeans established the European Union (EU) with a vision for peace and prosperity for the entire region. The EU has become an example of the connectedness of nations, probably with no possibility of war, leading to lasting regional peace. It has been a trendsetter with its model of regional cooperation, of actively sharing the core competencies of nations and, above all, of working for stability and peace. Global bodies have to work for regional cooperation like the EU in the interest of a more stable world.

SINGAPORE

On the other hand is the example of a small island nation, Singapore. It is a country with no natural resources other than its citizens. Its people of knowledge and skill have made Singapore an economically developed nation. Its leaders too reflect the virtues of its population. They have been men of integrity and sacrifice.

Lee Kuan Yew, who was the first prime minister of Singapore, from 1959 to 1990, provided creative leadership and made Singapore a great and integrated multicultural nation with a single mission, that is, Singapore itself. Under his leadership, Singapore became an economically developed nation and, above all, developed a unique culture wherein its citizens take pride in their country and obey the laws of the land.

THE UNITED STATES OF AMERICA

The US as we know it is only about 250-odd years old but there is much to learn from it. Take, for instance, its democratic temperament and its determination to come up with solutions to great natural, economic and other such challenges. The American vision and dream have been internalized by all its citizens. Every citizen wants America to be number one in the world. This attitude has resulted in the US's constant advancements and leadership in all fields, including technology, science, culture and the arts.

The US is another example of how a great nation is made by

great leaders. Visionary men and women give a nation direction
and stability. Thomas Jefferson and George Washington gave
the US its strong democratic foundation. Abraham Lincoln put
an end to slavery – even at the cost of his own life. If Dr Mandela
carried forward the fight against racial injustice started by
Mahatma Gandhi in South Africa, leaders like Martin Luther
King Jr were influenced by his principles in the same context
in the US. These are great leaders who shaped their countries,
and their assassinations echoed around the world, assisting
movements for freedom and justice everywhere.

INDIA

Lastly, let's come to India. India and the US have many
similarities despite their many differences. Unlike the US,
India is a civilization that goes back many thousands of years.
Again, unlike the US, India witnessed several invasions over the
centuries because of its climate and natural riches. But today
both are modern, multicultural, multi-religious and multilingual
democratic societies.

Dynasties from around the world ruled India through the
centuries. But the invaders imbibed the Indian ethos even as
the society absorbed the best of the traits of other civilizations.
It witnessed much violence but is now known as the land of
non-violence. Such is the impact that the creative leadership of
an individual – whether Emperor Ashoka or Mahatma Gandhi
– can have on the national character.

India is a great nation in many ways. It stands shoulder to

shoulder with the many nations discussed here. It has a rich culture that is widely respected around the world. It has had many inspiring leaders. It has produced greats in science and technology, philosophy and the arts. But India has some way to go before it is counted among the great nations of the twenty-first century.

And the pathway to that greatness starts with something very basic.

TWO

BACK TO THE BASICS

I HAVE WALKED the streets of many villages and towns and cities in India. I have also visited around twenty countries, where too I have done a fair bit of walking. There is one contrast I have observed between our nation and the others. More people walk here compared to those. The second contrast is that the citizens of the other countries take the responsibility for not littering the roads. The civic authorities there also ensure that there are sufficient waste bins on the roads and they are regularly cleared. Even densely populated cities such as Tokyo and Hong Kong fare well in terms of cleanliness because of strict laws and training to citizens of all ages. But that is not the case in India.

How can we hope to be considered a great nation if we ignore the basics of cleanliness and hygiene, toilets and sanitation? It is a problem of great magnitude. Across our villages and cities, even in our biggest urban centres, we see a shortage of toilets. Where toilets do exist, they are dirty and ill maintained, with improper drainage systems that create smelly surroundings and breeding grounds for insects and diseases.

Everyone understands the enormity of the problem and the impact it has on the public. But lasting solutions require dedicated teamwork between the government, the public and private sectors, non-governmental organizations (NGO) and the people. There are different dimensions such as hygiene education, integrated action between agencies to create and maintain facilities, cost effectiveness and continuous monitoring and improvement.

Good sanitary conditions and infrastructure are important indicators of the state of development of any nation. Can we transform India into a country known for its hygiene and good sanitary practices? The question has weighed on my mind for a long time.

In 2007, I had the privilege of addressing the World Toilet Summit – an annual event organized by the World Toilet Organization – that took place in New Delhi that year. A large number of national and international delegates from more than forty-one countries exchanged ideas to devise strategies and approaches required to improve sanitation coverage in different parts of the globe. There I had the occasion to dwell on this issue at some length and I would like to share the ideas that came up.

KEERAPALAYAM EXPERIENCE

In August 2004, I visited the Keerapalayam panchayat in Tamil Nadu's Cuddalore district. The office holders informed me that every one of the 1,125 dwelling units in the panchayat had sanitary facilities. Also, it was interesting to find that the women in the village had acquired masonry and plumbing skills, and had been responsible for constructing the household toilets. They had not only constructed toilets for the houses in their panchayat but also gone to neighbouring villages and provided their services. This had created new employment opportunities for the women and also enabled the panchayat to be tidy and free from diseases arising out of poor sanitary conditions.

Similar results were also reported by the Thamaraikulam panchayat in the state's Ramanathapuram district. I am sure that there are a number of isolated examples of this nature in the villages, towns and cities of our country. But this so-called 'simple' subject has long evaded solutions that can be replicated across the country. With India's ever-increasing population and the overcrowding of habitats, the problem has attained monumental proportions. We need to make an integrated effort to solve it in an accelerated way.

THE SOLUTION

The reality is that Keerapalayam and Thamaraikulam are exceptions in India. The general picture of toilets and sanitation is grim. And we have no one but ourselves to blame. We look around and see the primitive condition of toilets in schools, colleges, railway stations and public places, and we think that this is a situation that cannot be changed and one we need to live with. That has become our mindset. But it doesn't have to be this way.

The solution lies in spreading awareness about the problem and what we can do to address it. We need to start with our homes and primary schools. We need to intensify efforts to educate children about the need for hygienic toilets at homes, public places and in our public transport networks. Local citizen groups have to be energized to facilitate this education and to enable and monitor actions.

In this respect, I have come across the work of M.R. Raju of Peddapuram in Andhra Pradesh, who has undertaken the task of training rural children at the age of three in his nursery. His training includes inculcating in them good habits related to sanitation and nutrition. Such training is needed in all our schools.

INTEGRATED MISSION FOR SANITATION AND DRINKING WATER

In India's cities, towns and metros, the problem is inadequacy of facilities. In rural areas, it is one of lack of facilities, education and empowerment. It is indeed a national problem. If one looks at the allocations and plans in place, they are not insignificant. But the question that comes up is why there is no improvement in the situation in proportion to the resources being pumped in.

For instance, India's annual investment in water supply and sanitation is $5 (about Rs 350) per capita. The level of investment, even if it is low by international standards, has increased since the first decade of the twenty-first century. Access has also increased. Rural sanitation coverage was estimated at 1 per cent in 1980 but reached 21 per cent in 2008. The share of Indians with access to improved sources of water increased from 72 per cent in 1990 to 88 per cent by 2008. At the same time, only two Indian cities have continuous water supply and about 69 per cent Indians still lack access to improved sanitation facilities.

The problem is that the responsibility for water supply and sanitation at the central and state levels is shared by various ministries. At the central level, there are three ministries: the Ministry of Drinking Water and Sanitation (responsible for rural areas), the Ministry of Housing and Urban Poverty Alleviation and the Ministry of Urban Development (responsible for urban areas). But water supply and sanitation is a state subject under the Constitution. Central ministries only have an advisory capacity and a limited role in funding. Sector policy is a prerogative of state governments. A coherent integration of different agencies with the sole aim of ensuring that the benefits reach the stakeholders is the crux of the issue.

There is also a need for an effective measuring tool to assess the efficacy of the existing systems. For example, when sanitation improves, people's health should also improve. I consider that there is a direct relationship between the availability of modern sanitary systems and a reduction in the number of acute diarrhoea cases, for instance.

SOCIAL PARTICIPATION

At the same time, it must be said that creating and providing good sanitation facilities is not the responsibility of the government alone. It is equally a responsibility of the elected representatives of panchayati raj institutions (PRI), NGOs and the civil society. We need to focus on mobilizing all sections of society as sanitation can be provided to all only if that is done.

Mahatma Gandhi used to lay emphasis on strengthening local self-governments to solve various problems. Both issues of sanitation and local self-government were very close to his heart. Without the involvement of PRIs, the mission of total sanitation cannot be achieved. It is essential that gram panchayats play a pivotal role in sanitation promotion as they reflect the will of the people at the grass-roots level.

The involvement of women is also very important. Self-help groups, mahila samakhya (education for women's equality) and women's groups should be encouraged to take up sanitation and suitable incentives should be given to them. I have personally witnessed the success of such an approach and of women's participation in villages like Keerapalayam.

RAILWAY TOILETS

The condition of the toilets in our trains needs urgent attention and action. The primary aim should be to ensure that excreta is not discharged on to the tracks. Also, it is essential to make the new toilet systems cost-effective as we need lakhs of them for our trains. The railways may consider the introduction or modification of bogies to have modern urinals, toilets, wash basins and disposal systems so that the tracks stay clean and passengers are able to travel in a pleasant environment.

Urgent and coordinated action between railway authorities, researchers and production agencies is necessary to finalize the new design and system so that they can be incorporated immediately in our trains.

WHAT DO YOU WANT TO BE REMEMBERED FOR?

I generally assume that most NGOs have a purpose and would like to contribute to the welfare of society. Every NGO should ask itself, 'What do I want to be remembered for?' In this respect, I can see that Sulabh International will be remembered for the development and implementation of technologies and its work in the fields of sanitation, public toilets, recycling and the use of biogas. I would request Sulabh International, other NGOs and rural development agencies to take up work in places like Bihar, Uttar Pradesh and the north-eastern states. There is great scope for them to showcase their societal and entrepreneurial spirit and mission-oriented approach, and assist in rural transformation.

Let us imagine that it has rained for a couple of hours in a village. The rain creates many streams. Whether the water in the streams reaches the local lakes and ponds where it is stored for future use, or it goes to the sea, or it dries up on the way – it all depends on the paths created by the village panchayat for the flow of water. In some places, the roads are kept at a higher level so that the water there directly flows into the nearby water bodies. I have seen this in Mount Abu in Rajasthan.

In my long public life, I have had several opportunities to see the progress of works being carried out by NGOs in different places. Often sanitation facilities are created on single-pit toilets. As soon as the pit fills up, the toilet becomes unusable. Hence, we have to ensure that a sustainable mechanism is created for continuous functioning even if the NGO or government agency leaves the place. This should be done by training the local people so that they can manage the scheme and ensure that the benefits flow to the villagers continuously. This responsibility could be given to ex-servicemen after a certain amount of training as they come from a force known for its discipline and they are present in all parts of the country.

Life is an excellent opportunity. There is no great challenge in treading the well-laid-out path. Rural NGOs have to create new paths and be remembered for the creation of beautiful and clean villages across India.

CLOSED-LOOP SYSTEM OF WASTE MANAGEMENT

When I think of sanitation, the first thing that comes to mind is the provision of facilities with adequate water for all households in a village cluster. This can be a wealth-generating activity for the village. For example, in some villages, toilet facilities have been made out of fibreglass by local self-help groups. I have seen the fabrication of toilet facilities by villagers in Keerapalayam and Vallam in Tamil Nadu and Ahmedabad in Gujarat.

As a second step, it is to be ensured that all the toilets are functional at all times. This means conducting training in plumbing and maintenance of toilets by a group of professionals who can provide the service to the villagers for a fee. Third, continuous availability of water in the toilets needs to be ensured. With water resources depleting, this can be possible only if there is a system of recycling and recharging toilet water, including a linkage to water harvesting, in every home.

Fourth, there is a need to connect individual toilets to a common sewerage system for centralized disposal, without which all the efforts made towards providing hygienic toilet facilities in individual dwellings may not yield the desired results. I have come across a model executed by H.G.S. Gill, a non-resident Indian, at Karodi village in Punjab's Hoshiarpur district. He has used a technology which connects individual toilets to a central village sewerage system, carrying the waste to a remote location through an underground closed drainage system. There is an open sewerage tank exposed to the sun where the waste is separated from the water. The sewerage water is treated and used for agricultural purposes. Mr Gill ensures that individual households maintain their sanitation systems to prevent blockages, and that the central system is also maintained by specially trained staff. The central tank is cleaned after a few months and the solid waste converted into manure to be used for agricultural purposes. He has also extended this model to many more villages in Hoshiarpur.

What I want to emphasize here is that it is not enough to merely bring toilets to every house. It is essential to consider the overall problem of waste disposal and treatment so that the surroundings are kept clean at all times. There are seven requirements which should be fulfilled by a good toilet. I am told that the two-pit toilet satisfies all seven. In this system, after one pit fills up, it is not used for three years, during which time the other pit is used. Contents of the first pit turn into pathogen-free, odourless, solid manure in that time. It is then taken out by the beneficiaries and used for agricultural purposes.

The other type of waste in a village comes from animals, plants and trees, and what is created during cooking, processing, washing and other day-to-day activities. This can be categorized into biodegradable and non-biodegradable. The biodegradable waste can be converted into pellets and used for household heating, which otherwise requires fossil fuels. The biodegradable waste can also be used for vermicomposting. If the village has large amounts of biodegradable waste because of its human and animal population, it can also be used to generate electricity through biogas plants.

SANITATION AND TOILET INFRASTRUCTURE MISSION

I would suggest the following action plan to make total sanitation a success:

1. It is essential to evolve toilet systems for rural and urban India. The toilet systems should be considered an infrastructure rather than individual toilets for homes.

2. The sanitation and toilet infrastructure mission may include the construction of centralized tanks, treatment systems to convert the waste into manure and recycled water, the laying and extension of pipelines to every street, the construction of individual and community toilets, and connecting them with the main pipelines. Waste water outlets have to be interlinked to a storage system for waste water treatment and recycling. This model can be followed in new PURA (providing urban amenities in rural areas) developments, urban slums and public utility systems.

3. The toilets designed should be reliable, have a long life and have a flushing system that consumes less water. Individual toilet systems can also consider utilizing recycled water.

4. In rural areas, an eco-toilet system that uses the desiccating or composting model may be considered. But further research and development is required for the total elimination of smell and mechanical clearance of the manure after composting.

5. There is a need to integrate and bring synergy between different ministries such as the ministries of rural development, urban development, health, social justice and empowerment, and water resources.

6. Elected panchayat representatives should be trained and empowered to prepare overall plans for the toilet infrastructure of their respective villages, have a say in the choice of technologies, and create a maintenance and support services mechanism for the uninterrupted, reliable and failure-free operation of the toilet infrastructure in the

village. Every home and community toilet system should be connected to the infrastructure.

CONCLUSION

India is on a mission to transform itself into a developed nation by 2020. Sanitation and clean environment make up the foundation of that transformation. It should also have a direct impact on the health of the people, leading to significant reductions in jaundice, other waterborne diseases and malaria. There should be a monitoring system in place that checks whether the sanitation programme leads to a reduction in health care expenditure and the number of man-days lost by the citizens.

Thus, it can be seen that the sanitation programme makes good business sense if we convert it into a sanitation and toilet infrastructure mission.

THREE

LESSONS FROM MY TRAVELS

THROUGHOUT MY PROFESSIONAL life of about six decades, working in a spectrum of organizations and in varying capacities, I had the opportunity to traverse the length and breadth of the nation. During my presidential years too, from 2002 to 2007, I made it a point to visit India's rural areas and interact with and learn from the people I met. India's heart is in its villages. Just like a doctor begins his diagnosis by listening to the patient's heartbeat, the planning and execution of any policy in a nation of a billion people has to start with the learning derived from its 6,00,000 villages.

TUENSANG, NAGALAND, OCTOBER 2002

I recall my visit to Nagaland, amidst the fading eastern end of the mighty Himalayas, in October 2002. It is a state small in size but very rich in biodiversity and culture. It has a population of about 2.5 million, largely tribal, and many different dialects and cultures unique to the tribes. One of the places I visited there was Tuensang. It is Nagaland's largest district and it is strategically important as it is on the border between India and Myanmar. While I was there, I participated in a tribal council meeting of the nearby areas.

Nagaland's tribal leaders are special people who are not only the political representatives of their people but also the custodians of their unique culture. They all came in their traditional colourful and vibrant attire, each armed with a bunch of papers with their agendas written by hand on them. I was told that they generally preferred to sit in the shade of a large tree in the open but had decided to conduct the meeting in a closed room as the visiting dignitary was the President of India. They greeted me, then each other and professionally took their seats around a circle. The discussions began in utmost seriousness. The agenda for the day was how the tribal council's initiatives had augmented the productivity of vegetables and fruits.

'I am happy to announce that production now exceeds demand by a large margin for the first time!' someone said.

People applauded. I too was happy to note the brilliant performance of the villages.

But then a young leader got up and said, 'Respected members, while it is good news that the productivity and quality have both gone up, the question is: how do we build an economically viable model?'

Someone in a corner then had an idea. 'We need to find what markets we can export to,' she said. 'I have a small team which can study the demand patterns of nearby villages and urban areas. We should explore these options.' Everyone agreed with her.

Then a senior tribal started speaking as others listened with respect and interest. 'Mr President and my fellow council members,' he said, 'there is one major hurdle, which is the non-availability of roads between villages and urban areas. We also do not have vehicles to transport our goods.'

The absorbing discussion went on for an hour about this problem. After many ideas were thrown up and discussed, they took the decision to form a cooperative society to buy the excess vegetables and fruits and bear the responsibility of hiring a swift and robust mode of transport to take the produce across difficult terrain to faraway markets and even beyond the borders of Nagaland. They then discussed how to improve the tourism industry in the region and prepared a memorandum for the chief minister, asking him to construct a number of helipads to improve access to tourist destinations and also to help transport excess agricultural produce.

NICOBAR ISLAND, JANUARY 2005

I saw this situation playing out – lack of physical access impeding economic activity – in a number of remote tribal areas in the country. In January 2005, when I visited the Nicobar Island after the devastating tsunami the previous month, I met some tribal leaders there. I asked them why they were not using the wealth of the ocean for their economic growth.

'There is so much of marine wealth at your disposal,' I said to them. 'Fishermen from the neighbouring countries are illegally exploiting our seas. Why don't you use this national resource?'

The tribal leaders thought about my question and then responded. They were of the unanimous view that while they had deep traditional knowledge about fishing, they did not know how to market and sell the excess fish outside their villages. They also wanted to understand the technology for fish processing. This lack of knowledge hindered their economic growth.

Before leaving for Nicobar, I had been told in New Delhi that the tsunami had swallowed several parents and rendered their children orphans. But on the island I noticed a curious absence of orphanages. 'When I visited Andaman, I saw three orphanages constructed after the tsunami,' I said to the leaders. 'What about Nicobar?'

They told me – to my great surprise, and like a silver lining in the destruction left behind by the tsunami – that there were 'no orphans here'. One senior but very energetic leader told me after deep thought, 'The children who are left without surviving parents are indeed the children of every home. We don't need orphanages. Our homes are taking care of these children. After all, we are one big family on this little island.'

Such a beautiful custom – of transmitting love, of caring and of compassion – is indeed inspiring and needs to be preserved and nurtured across the nation and the world. When we talk of development, this aspect has to be kept in mind.

WAYANAD, KERALA, FEBRUARY 2011

Let me take you some 1,200 km to the west to Kerala. On 17 February 2011, I was invited to inaugurate a unique education programme by the Wayanad district education department and, later in the day, I was also scheduled to interact with students from various schools at the Jawahar Navodaya Vidyalaya. A few of my colleagues and I were supposed to leave Delhi at 9.30 a.m. for Bangalore and then board a connecting flight to Calicut, reaching there around 3.30 p.m. before driving to Wayanad to reach the venue of the function at 5 p.m. Everything was perfectly planned – but then the most meticulously detailed plans sometimes fall victim to the most unforeseen snags.

We reached Delhi airport on time, only to be informed that the flight to Bangalore had been delayed due to 'unavoidable' circumstances. Our first impression was that the delay would be a matter of a few minutes, until one hour passed, then another, and then another, while we waited in the airport waiting room, trying to best utilize our time by refining the lectures and reading books. We finally reached Bangalore at 5.30 p.m. Of course, our connecting flight had departed long back. I was anxious for the children and others who were waiting in Wayanad and immediately called up the organizers to explain the situation.

To my surprise, they all said, 'Sir, none of us will move

from here. We will wait for you even if it means waiting here all night. We know you will not disappoint us.'

I was moved and was determined to reach Wayanad whichever way possible. We discussed the various possibilities and concluded that the only way was to travel by road, through the dense Kerala forests, across hundreds of kilometres, and reach Wayanad in about six hours. I looked at my wristwatch. It was 6 p.m. then – which meant that our best hope was to reach Wayanad by midnight. I decided to take the option and conveyed my decision to the organizers.

Thus began one of my longest single-stretch road journeys. Within about 100 km, except the road, all the typical markers of human civilization vanished, giving way to a lush green forest with its own unique sights and sounds. In the moonlit night we could see the long shadows cast by the lights of our vehicle. The sound of the engine was occasionally matched by the trumpeting of elephants. The forest wealth was immense and bore testimony to the great national asset we possess.

After the long non-stop journey, during which we spent more than six-and-a-half hours on the road, we were finally greeted by a signboard that read, 'Welcome to Wayanad'. Mobile connectivity was available again, and man-made lights twinkled against the backdrop of the stars in the night sky as we entered the town. We went straight to the venue of the first function, the Chandragiri auditorium.

A loud cheer went up as soon as we reached, and I was astonished to see that more than 2,000 people had filled up the hall to greet me. I was deeply touched by the gesture and moved by the thought of the hardships they must have endured while waiting for me late into the night. India is a unique country and the people here are like no other. When we are driven by some purpose or mission, Indians in any part of the nation can do unimaginable things. What I saw in Wayanad was one small example of this.

While at the function, I inaugurated the Arividam Programme for spreading education in the district. Arividam means a place of knowledge and information. Knowledge makes an individual great, so the objective of the programme is to evolve great citizens for the state of Kerala. It is to deliver education, information and knowledge to students, teachers and the public to bridge the digital gap in education at the regional level. This includes the creation of videoconferencing facilities for principals, headmasters and officials; individual websites for all schools; and the creation of people's networks.

Information technology and computers, coupled with innovative planning and execution, can be a wonderful tool for taking knowledge to the masses. Applications like Facebook have reached millions of users. Why can we not use the same philosophy and technology to reach a large rural audience with education and knowledge?

After this function I swiftly arrived, full of energy, at 2.30 a.m. at Jawahar Navodaya Vidyalaya, where thousands of children from Wayanad had gathered. It was an extraordinary hour for a meeting but they were surprisingly attentive. After the function, one student asked, 'Sir, how can science and technology help remove illiteracy?' Of course, a couple of hours ago, I had come across one good example to tell him about: Arividam.

URI, URSA AND TANGDHAR, JAMMU AND KASHMIR, OCTOBER 2005

From Kerala let me move to Kashmir. In October 2005, a severe earthquake caused massive destruction of life and property in the Kashmir Valley. I visited the regions of Uri, Ursa and Tangdhar, all of which are on the border between India and Pakistan, to take stock of the large-scale rescue and rehabilitation work being carried out there.

I also attended a meeting of locals, largely farmers, and representatives of the government, including the governor, the chief minister and senior officers from the armed forces. At the meeting I recalled my visit to the three regions the previous day, particularly the lack of means of livelihood that I had observed. I asked the locals why they did not grow fruits in their farms, especially apples, for which Kashmir is known around the world.

'Sir, we don't have land. Our land is with the army,' they said.

Their answer surprised me and caught some of the officials accompanying me off guard. I looked at the governor, the chief minister and the senior officers from the army and air force. There was an uncomfortable silence. I knew I had to respond to this issue. Understanding the difficulty of the locals, I said that it was essential to earmark some land for cultivation in the border areas so that we could bring economic prosperity to the region. I further stressed the need to establish proper linkages to markets. India's security concerns should not impede the development of our border regions. In fact, development is the best answer to any form of societal unrest.

KIBITHU, ARUNACHAL PRADESH, MARCH 2007

In 2007, the last year of my presidency, army chief General Joginder Jaswant Singh urged me to visit India's border with China in Arunachal Pradesh. The general, popularly known as JJ, is an army veteran with a strong, overwhelming personality and an evergreen smile. So, when he insisted that I should address our soldiers at the border, I readily obliged.

We arrived at a place called Kibithu where Chinese and Indian territories meet. We were in a valley, surrounded by mountains piercing the skies. On the other side I could see the Chinese posts, situated a little higher than ours. A few curious soldiers had gathered, probably attracted by the commotion caused by our visit. I looked at our young soldiers and locals who had assembled there and then at the Himalayas towering above. I was touched by the hardships the soldiers braved in the difficult conditions. No matter what support systems we create for them, the hard reality of the Himalayan battlefield is that the weather is often the bigger adversary than the soldiers of the neighbouring country.

Then I looked at the locals assembled, largely tribals. Their cheerful faces and smiles did not conceal the most obvious signs of poverty and hardship – overworked hands, worn-out clothes and frail bodies. The dwellers of India's frontier regions face terrible hardships daily, often without any special support, and perform a number of auxiliary and logistical roles for the army. As I walked past them, I heard the usual enthusiastic greeting in these tribal areas: 'Jai Hind'.

I then addressed the integrated army command, with all the soldiers and officers, and I saw in them a surprising enthusiasm for their work in spite of the difficult conditions and an ever-readiness to face any challenges – be it the weather or the threats from across the border. I met a number of young officers after my address to them.

'I realize that you are working day and night for the peace and safety of the nation and its people,' I said to them. 'I am proud of you all. Can you share with me one of your most cherished dreams?'

There was a moment of silence and then several enthusiastic hands went up.

A young soldier rose up and gave me a smart salute. 'Sir!' he said loudly. 'Whenever I see the Chinese placed higher up in the Himalayas, I am reminded of my visit to Tawang. My utmost ambition is to fight and win any instance of aggression by the Chinese.'

Another young officer added, 'Sir, my ambition for life is to recover the 50,000 sq km of land belonging to us back from Chinese possession. I will fight till my last breath for that.'

The locals burst into applause and started chanting, 'Jai Hind! Jai Hind!' at the top of their voices. I was amazed by the spirit and the resolve of the officers, soldiers and the locals. We need to nurture these regions and this spirit.

BHADARIYA, RAJASTHAN, MAY 1998

From the far east of the nation, let us now move across the length of India, some 3,000 km to the west. It was 15 May 1998. India had just successfully conducted five nuclear tests, on 11 and 13 May, elevating its defence stature. The nation was jubilant. My team of scientists and I were returning from Pokhran in Rajasthan, the site of the tests. Pokhran is far into the Thar desert where little life exists. Those days of May were particularly hot, with temperatures soaring over 50°C as the sun beat down, making the sand shimmer.

On our way back, meandering on the desert roads, we came across a small village called Bhadariya. Seeing the signboard announcing its name, the eyes of one of my colleagues immediately lit up. He said he knew the place, adding that he had heard of a famous ashram there. On his request, we decided to take a small detour and visit the place.

Bhadariya is a small hamlet. While it was not difficult to locate the ashram, it was hard to believe what we saw there. It was a large place, bursting with greenery in the middle of the desert. The head priest of the ashram, Baba Sri Bhadariya Maharaj, greeted us and asked whether we would like to see the unique library he had created. He took us down a staircase to an underground chamber which led to the library.

We were pleasantly surprised to find the room remarkably cool. Baba Sri Bhadariya Maharaj told us that the design of the building was such that the library would be naturally air-conditioned even if the outside temperature was high. The walls were lined with thousands of books on different subjects, in different languages and relating to different periods in history. Some of them were even handwritten on parchment. Baba Sri Bhadariya Maharaj presented to us books which were hundreds of years old and told us that the ashram had conserved traditional knowledge from ages ago.

While we were reading in the library, mesmerized by the cultural wealth, he brought us huge glasses of milk. 'Baba, in the middle of this desert, where do you get such delicious fresh milk from?' I asked him.

He smiled and asked me to follow him. He then led me to a huge cowshed, with hundreds of cows, behind the ashram. 'Kalam,' he said, 'these are all abandoned cows. People drove them away when they stopped giving milk. For them these cows were useless. But, you see, just like you, I am also a technologist,' he laughed. 'I have a special method of treating the same stray cows, and today they are all healthy and happy and produce large quantities of quality milk – which you hold in your glass.'

I was amazed to see such a noble mission in action. 'But Baba,' I said, 'where do you find fodder for all these animals?'

He then asked me to sit down on a small cot in the shade of a tree and told me the story of Bhadariya's transformation. 'Years ago,' he started, 'the people of this place were very poor and addicted to different types of intoxicants, including liquor, cigarettes and other forms of local weed. This place was barren. There were several social problems like poverty, hunger, lack of health care and malnutrition. Water was scarce and yet poorly managed. Look at what we then did, with cooperation and support from the villagers. We started a de-addiction campaign, right here in the ashram, which is now spread to over seventy villages around Bhadariya. We executed a mission of greening Bhadariya and its surroundings with the help of locals by planting lakhs of trees. We had tube wells dug, and agriculture started in this place – with special ways to conserve water.

'This ashram also provides knowledge on naturopathy and herbal medicines to the rural community and treats their cattle,' Baba continued passionately. 'You know, Kalam, the villagers are so happy about all this that they provide fodder for these cows. Of course, when the cows start giving milk, I give milk and butter free of cost to the needy and the travellers passing through this place ... like yourself, Kalam!' he added as an afterthought and laughed once again as he refilled my glass.

'One final question, Baba,' I said. 'Where does all this knowledge about local herbs, rehabilitating cows and other things come from?'

Baba's eyes reflected the bright sunlight of the desert and he smiled as he pointed to the underground library. 'From there!' he said.

Bhadariya is a small place in the middle of the Thar desert but has a great lesson for the world. It is an example of integrated development – of communication, dissemination of knowledge, medical care, cattle rearing and fodder management, all taking place together in this desert to transform land, resources and human life using local and traditional knowledge, coupled with modern science and technology. This is a fundamental aspect of the pathways to greatness which we will discuss in this book, and it is valid not just for one nation or a group of nations but for the entire global community.

FOUR

Hand in Hand

WHAT IS TRUE of Bhadariya is true of society in general too. Different facets of life have to come together and work in synergy for overall growth and development. All the different systems at play have to work with a common vision. It has to be transparent and pure – only then can there be an integrated solution with a focus on development. The problems that plague our nation are complex, but the common goal of national development can provide objectivity and lead to appropriate, timely solutions. I would like to explain how every system needs to function for a single purpose with integrity.

1. Political Leaders

Political leaders should set an example for civil society by articulating a vision for the nation and engaging in development politics. There is a need for political leaders to respect the laws of the land and ensure that political power is not used to circumvent them.

2. LAWMAKERS

There is a need to simplify the law, discard irrelevant and old acts with a certain periodicity. The system should be such that the dispensation of justice is fast and fair. Our education system should promote legal literacy through formal and informal mechanisms, particularly for the rural community.

3. CITIZENS

Citizens should have respect for others' rights. They should use the legal system for good purposes and not for petty, selfish ends. Moreover, feedback from citizens is most valuable in a democratic system, and their vigilance in selecting the right type of representatives helps create conditions conducive to growth.

4. ADMINISTRATION

The administration should be responsive, proactive and also innovative to keep pace with the changes in society and people's expectations. Administrators should make greater use of technology like e-governance to execute decisions fast.

5. POLICE

The police should function in a way that inspires the faith of good citizens in the system and they have nothing to fear. They should not succumb to any external pressures in the delivery of justice. They should protect honest officials in discharging their duties. Police personnel should be given perks and remuneration consistent with their performance expectations.

6. SCIENTISTS AND TECHNOLOGISTS

Scientists and technologists have to be partners in the development process and bring about innovative solutions for accelerated growth. There is also a need to communicate and explain science and technology at all levels to pave the way for fast decision-making.

7. LAWYERS

The legal profession is not a mere business but bears the responsibility for truth and justice to prevail. Its practitioners should abide by their professional ethics. Law schools should instil such values in lawyers from the very outset of their careers so that they become role models for the youth when they occupy senior positions.

8. JUDGES

It is essential to make truth prevail irrespective of the stature of the affected parties. The speed of delivery of justice is crucial. While deterrent laws, good role models and moral education at a young age can help reduce crime, timely delivery of justice will make the public less cynical about the system.

9. Media

The media should remain vigilant and proactive. However, they should be cautious not to prejudge issues or sacrifice truth for the sake of sensationalism.

10. Artists and Writers

Practitioners of the liberal arts, in addition to uniting minds across the country and continuously enriching the heritage and showcasing the potential of the country, have the power to express independent, issue-based opinions in the best democratic traditions.

11. Non-governmental and Welfare Organizations

Non-governmental bodies are known for their zealous social commitment and can bring about visible changes with their hard work, integrity and honesty.

~

All of us as citizens, irrespective of the profession to which we belong, have to regulate ourselves by a code of behaviour ordained by the Constitution. We should always act with discretion and be circumspect about our actions. I voice this thought as a citizen who is concerned about the denial of the fruits of the rule of law to others who are less privileged. Privileges are meant to be enjoyed with prudence by those on whom they are conferred; they are not meant to make others suffer. Certainly, they are not meant to be flaunted. Rights are meant to be exercised to achieve the right thing; they are not to be brandished. Politeness and moderation are virtues to be inculcated by each one of us.

As for the pillars of our democracy – namely, the legislature, the executive and the judiciary – the sooner they realize that one cannot live without the other two for a healthy and dynamic society, the better for all of us. We should strive to see real democracy blossom by nurturing citizens' aspirations and creating an environment in which they can be realized. That would be the best prescription for a healthy and resurgent democratic system.

I would like to recall here something I observed after a talk in the US in May 2013. I had addressed a group of people on the topic of 'Evolving a World without War' in Maryland at the Jagadguru Sri Shivarathreeswara (JSS) institutions. During my interaction with the audience, I noted that the questions and suggestions of the American citizens pertained to my talk whereas the Indian members of the audience asked me general questions unrelated to my presentation. The message is that we as a people need to develop a habit of listening to the speaker and shaping our questions according to his or her talk so that we contribute to the discussion in a productive manner.

What this incident led me to think is whether we, as a nation, are asking ourselves the right questions. Do we go into abstractions instead of addressing a problem? We offer solutions that will see the light of day five years down the line, but nothing immediate. We talk of space exploration but do not fix the road beneath our feet.

It is important to ask the right questions for a nation's economic development to make it competitive. Competitiveness is powered by knowledge. Knowledge is powered by technology. Technology is powered by innovation. In a knowledge society, we have to make innovations continuously. Innovation opens up new vistas of knowledge and adds new dimensions to our imagination to make everyday life more meaningful and richer in depth and content. Innovation is born out of creativity. And creativity comes from beautiful minds.

One can find beautiful minds in any part of the world – a fishing hamlet or a farmer's household, classrooms or laboratories, industries or R&D centres. Creativity is a process through which we can continuously improve ideas and find unique solutions by making gradual alterations and refinements in our work. The important aspect of creativity is seeing the same thing as everybody else does but thinking of something different. Innovation and creativity ultimately result in a culture of excellence – a beautiful nation born out of beautiful minds.

FIVE

A Beautiful Nation

THINK OF A traveller standing at a pass high up in the Himalayas, looking out at the entire country spread out before him. What does he see? A landscape full of variety, with trees, plants and creatures of every description; rivers and streams sweeping out to the seas that surround the land mass on three sides; deserts and rocky mountain ranges; thick forests of sal and a hundred other tree species; a people with a diverse culture, speaking different tongues, with a literature that could occupy a scholar for many lifetimes and, above all, a welcoming, warm and engaging disposition. The land mass is not all. The diverse beauty of the country continues in the Bay of Bengal, 1,300 km away from the mainland, on the Andaman and Nicobar Islands, and in the Arabian Sea, 450 km from the mainland, in Lakshadweep.

Alongside this plenitude of beauty, though, the traveller will also see many discouraging things that can easily be corrected: increasing pollution of the rivers; deforestation; towns and cities growing haphazardly in the midst of unsanitary conditions and festering garbage; neglect and deprivation; a lack of basics like health and education across large swathes of the population, and so on. The worst of the evils he will observe will be poverty, illiteracy and unemployment, which drive the forces of anger and violence, making the society unstable.

The stability of any society is a vital factor that decides peace. It revolves around the provision of basic needs such as food, clothing, shelter, and safety and security. Every human being in this country has a right to these basic needs, to live with dignity, to aspire for distinction. The availability of opportunities to resort to just and fair means in order to attain this dignity and distinction is what democracy is all about. That is what our Constitution is all about. And that is what makes life wholesome and worth living in a true and vibrant democracy.

At this point I would like to remind all of us that it is necessary to work for the unity of minds in society for the smooth functioning of our democracy. The increasing intolerance for others' views and way of life – and the expression of this intolerance through lawless violence against people – cannot be justified in any context. All of us have to work hard and behave in a civilized manner in our day-to-day lives to ensure that the rights of our fellow citizens are protected. That is the very foundation of our democratic values. That is what will make India a beautiful nation.

ENLIGHTENED HUMAN BEINGS

How can we evolve enlightened human beings to achieve that goal? The answer lies in small acts performed daily. When a child is empowered by its parents in the various phases of its growth, the child is transformed into a responsible citizen. When a teacher is empowered with knowledge and experience, human beings with good value systems emerge. When people are empowered with technology, they are able to realize their potential. When the leader of any institution empowers his or her people, more leaders are in turn created who can change the nation in multiple areas. When women are empowered, a more equal society is assured. When political leaders empower the people through visionary policies, the prosperity of the nation is certain. When religions are empowered so that each one of them becomes a spiritual force, peace and happiness will blossom in people's hearts. Such empowerment alone can create enlightened citizens with a sound value system.

I believe that there are essentially three elements that go into creating enlightened human beings: education with a good value system, integration of capacities, and removal of societal discrimination.

1. Education with a Good Value System

The most important part of a person's life is his childhood. The learning our young citizens receive at home, in school and in society between the ages of five and sixteen will shape them for the rest of their lives. During this phase, they need a good value-based education to become enlightened human beings. This reminds me of the words of an ancient Greek teacher: 'Give me a child for seven years. Afterwards, let God or devil take the child. They cannot change the child.'

Parents and teachers need to have an integrated mission: education with a good value system – at home and in school. If children miss out on this value-based education of 25,000 hours, we cannot establish a society marked by its integrity. Education is fundamental to building the nation of our dreams. All our aspirations as a society are tied to the capabilities of our youngsters, who form such a large part of our population. Dr Sarvepalli Radhakrishnan, the second President of India, once said, 'Education should be imparted with a view to the type of society that we wish to build. We are working for a modern democracy built on the values of human dignity and equality. These are only ideals; we should make them living forces. Our vision of the future should include these great principles.'

A child's individuality and creativity need to be given due importance in our education. The curriculum needs to be innovative and the examination system overhauled so that it recognizes and evaluates creativity and new thinking rather than the memorization of facts. Schools must move away from being centres of education alone, instead becoming centres of knowledge and skill development.

This reminds me of some incidents from my own life. My teacher in class eight, way back in 1943, was Shri Sivasubramania Iyer. He was a great human being who taught us science and other subjects. One day he was teaching us how birds fly. He told us about the importance of the shape of the bird, how it flaps its wings, how it gains momentum, and how the tail gives it direction. He explained it well but somehow we could not visualize the process. Then, I remember, it was 3.30 p.m. He took us to the shore of our Rameswaram island. And there, at sunset, we saw the sea birds fly. We watched them flap their wings, gather momentum, take flight and change direction with their tails. That was the day I knew what I would do. I would study the science of flight. My teacher, his life and his way of teaching showed me the way. In that class I decided my mission.

The other incident took place when I was at St Joseph's College, Tiruchirappalli. A great mathematics professor called Totadri Iyengar taught there. He would radiate knowledge when he walked. Young students would look at him with awe and respect. I had a different mathematics professor, who was fondly called 'Calculus' Srinivasan. He too would talk about Prof. Iyengar with deep respect. When I was in the first year of my BSc course, Calculus Srinivasan selected me as one of his top ten students to be part of the Mathematics Club in college. The biggest benefit of being part of this club was a lecture series by Prof. Iyengar for the members. I still remember that day when Prof. Iyengar gave a one-hour lecture on India's ancient mathematicians and astronomers. It still rings in my ears as though it took place yesterday. He introduced me to Aryabhata, Bhaskara and, in our time, Ramanujam – pioneers in astronomy and mathematics and inspirational figures.

These two incidents became the foundation for my education, learning and value system.

Like him, our school and college teachers need to continuously assess and evaluate themselves to see how effective their teaching is in shaping the learning of their students.

2. Integration of Capacities

We need to give our children the capacity to contribute to economic development and nation-building. This in turn includes the capacity for research or inquiry, for creativity and innovation and for entrepreneurial leadership. Our children need to be able to integrate these different capacities to become enlightened human beings.

3. Removal of Societal Discrimination

Education also plays an important role in bringing about unity of minds and creating a sense of equality among the children who are the future of our nation. Teachers should strive to remove different forms of societal discrimination such as those based on social status and gender and economic disparity from their classrooms and from the minds of the children. They can do this by treating all children equally, without any bias, irrespective of whether the child is a boy or a girl, comes from a rich or poor family, or belongs to a particular region or religion.

HAPPY HOMES

The next step in creating a beautiful nation is the creation of beautiful homes. I believe that only united and happy homes can lead to the birth of a strong nation. A beautiful home has four dimensions:

1. The Habit of Reading

Let us look at a small home with a father, mother, son and daughter – or two sons or two daughters. In this home, both parents earn. I visualize, in this little home, a small library with at least ten great books. The parents should inculcate the habit of reading in their children by reading books to them at breakfast or dinner. The whole family should be together for at least one meal every day so that they communicate freely.

When they are all together at the dining table, either parent takes a book out of the small library and narrates a story based on ethical and moral values. The children listen to the story and then offer their comments on it. This routine motivates the children to read the book in detail, on their own, and put its lessons into practice in their day-to-day lives. Some children may also go to school and discuss such stories with other children, and this benefits the larger community.

This daily family get-together thus becomes a way of disseminating knowledge and ethical values into society over a period of time. The children who benefit from such practices will always be engaged in carrying out their responsibilities with excellence, dedication and self-esteem.

2. The Happiness of Mothers

The cornerstone of a happy home is a happy mother. She looks after and nurtures the entire family, so her well-being is of utmost importance. Whenever I meet our youth – be it in schools, colleges or universities – I urge them to take some time out every day to make their mothers happy. I administer an oath to them, which goes as follows:

From today onwards, I will make my mother happy.
If my mother is happy, my home is happy.
If my home is happy, the society will be happy.
If societies are happy, the state will be happy.
If the state is happy, the nation will be happy.

3. Transparent, Corruption-free Homes

There is a crying need in our nation to develop a transparent and corruption-free society. Corruption emanates from a few homes and we should make it our mission to curb it at home itself. We are a society of around 200 million families. Even if we assume that a third of them are corrupt, it means that approximately 60 million homes in India are corrupt in a big or small way.

But there is a way to change this situation. I urge the youth, if they sense the virus of corruption afflicting their families, to persuade their parents with their love and affection to not follow the path that will ruin our nation. My conscience says that more than any law, this movement of the youth will be effective against corruption.

4. Green Homes

Climate change is the biggest threat that the world faces today. Deforestation, industrialization and transportation are leading to increased heating of our planet. This is the cause of devastating and untimely floods and droughts around the world.

If all our homes take it upon themselves, they can definitely change the situation. Every home must take an oath to plant and nurture at least one tree. One fully grown tree absorbs 20 kg of carbon dioxide and emits 14 kg of oxygen. If every Indian home plants one tree and nurtures it, we will have over 200 million trees, which can definitely contain the climate change problem.

A BEAUTIFUL INDIA

Enlightened human beings and happy homes will go a long way in the creation of a beautiful India. Here I would like to share some thoughts on the evolution of a beautiful India that combines economic prosperity and a good value system drawn from our civilizational heritage. Economists all around the world have predicted that India will occupy pride of place in the world order by the year 2020. In the run-up to that landmark year, with the economic progress of the past few years behind us, we need to launch a major thrust to attain national prosperity. We need to work towards giving our future generations a competitive nation which has the following characteristics:

1. A nation that is prosperous, healthy, secure, peaceful and happy.
2. A nation where the rural–urban divide has reduced to a thin line.
3. A nation where there is an equitable distribution of energy and quality water.
4. A nation where agriculture, industry and the service sector work in symphony, absorbing technology, thereby resulting in sustained wealth generation leading to a higher employment potential.
5. A nation where education is not denied to any meritorious candidates because of societal or economic discrimination.
6. A nation which is the best destination for the most talented scholars and scientists all over the world.
7. A nation where the best of health care is available to the entire population.
8. A nation where governments use the best of technologies to be responsive, transparent, easily accessible and simple in their rules, and thereby free of corruption.

9. A nation where poverty has been totally alleviated, illiteracy and crime against women are eradicated, and no one in society feels alienated.

10. A nation that is one of the best places to live in on Earth and brings smiles to a billion faces.

SECTION II

OATHS

SIX

FOR THE YOUTH

AS A TEACHER, a scientist, a technologist and as the President of India, I have met millions of people from all walks of life. In Parliament and legislative assemblies I have met political leaders and members. In schools I met students and teachers. I have met doctors and paramedical staff in hospitals. During my travels to some of the remote parts of India, I have met tribal leaders. Wherever I have gone, I have administered oaths to the thousands of people I met, keeping in mind the group or profession they belong to. I believe that these oaths do influence their lives or bring about a change in them in some small way.

For instance, in an earlier chapter I wrote about my travel to Wayanad, Kerala, in February 2011. I had met students of the Jawahar Navodaya Vidyalaya there at 2.30 a.m. They were fresh and full of life even at that hour and happily took this ten-point oath that I administered:

1. I will have a goal and work hard to achieve it. I realize that having a small aim is a crime.
2. I will work with integrity and succeed with integrity.
3. I will be a good member of my family, of society, of the nation and of the world.
4. I will always try to save or improve someone's life without any discrimination because of their caste, creed, language, religion or state.
5. Wherever I am and whatever I do, I will always think, 'What can I give?'
6. I will always remember the importance of time. My motto will be: 'Let not my winged days be spent in vain.'
7. I will always work for a clean planet Earth and clean energy.
8. As a youth of my nation, I will work with courage to achieve success in all my tasks and enjoy the success of others.
9. I am as young as my faith and as old as my doubt. Hence, I will light the lamp of faith in my heart.
10. My national flag flies in my heart and I will bring glory to my nation.

A society must always give special attention to the dreams, concerns and aspirations of its youth because they are the ones who will shape its future. More than 40 per cent of India's population is below the age of twenty, according to the census data of 2011. I often say that the ignited minds of the youth are the most powerful resource on the earth, above the earth and under the earth. I am convinced that youth power, if properly directed and controlled, could bring about transformational changes in humanity for its progress, meeting its challenges and bringing about peace and prosperity.

Let us consider some of the major problems that the world faces. Two-thirds of its population lives in poverty, often without any access to safe drinking water, leave alone quality education. How can the youth of the world contribute to correct the situation? Can every educated person spread literacy to at least five people in his or her lifetime? Can the youth spread the message of water conservation? Can they come up with out-of-the-box solutions to different problems?

Some years ago I started the Lead India 2020 movement. It is indeed a youth movement, based on my ten-point oath for the youth and born out of my belief that the youth can make a difference to society in the areas of literacy, environment, social justice and minimizing the rural–urban divide. They can work for national development even as they work hard for an individual goal. I insist that having a small aim is a crime. A youth working towards a career goal can also simultaneously serve his family, the society, the nation and humanity as a whole. All are complementary.

There are some key principles, drawn from real-life anecdotes and the teachings of different religions and spiritual thinkers, on which my oath for the youth is based. Let me tell you the story behind them.

1. Save or Improve Someone's Life

Mahatma Gandhi's mother had once said to him: 'Son, in your entire lifetime, if you can save or improve someone's life, your birth as a human being and your life will be a success. You have the blessings of the Almighty God.' This advice had a deep impact on Gandhiji and made him work for humanity throughout his life.

2. Remove 'I' and 'Me' from Your Outlook

I happened to visit a 400-year-old Buddhist monastery in Tawang during a tour of Arunachal Pradesh in 2003. I was there for almost an entire day. I observed that the people of the nearby villages radiated happiness in spite of the severe winter. The monks of all age groups at the monastery seemed serene. I asked myself what it was about Tawang and the surrounding villages which allowed the people to be at peace with themselves. I then posed the question to the chief monk at the monastery.

He did not answer immediately. He smiled at me and said, 'You are the President of India. You must know all about us and the whole nation.'

'Please give me your thoughtful analysis,' I repeated. 'It is very important to me.'

Behind us was a beautiful golden image of Lord Buddha smiling and radiating peace. The chief monk assembled nearly a hundred young and experienced monks. He and I sat in their midst. He then gave a short discourse, which I would like to share with all of you.

'In the present world,' he began, 'we have a problem of distrust and unhappiness transforming into violence. This monastery spreads the message that when you remove "I" and "me" from your mind, you will eliminate your ego. If you get rid of your ego, your hatred of your fellow human beings will vanish. If hatred goes out of your mind, the violence in your thinking and actions will disappear. If the violence in your mind goes away, peace will spring in its place. Then peace and peace alone will blossom in society.'

That is how I came to understand the beautiful formula for a peaceful life. The most important, and also difficult, part of it is for an individual to remove 'I' and 'me' from his thinking. For this, the teachings of our ancient philosophers need to be inculcated in our children at a young age.

3. Forgiveness

In Tawang I received one part of the answer to my question, 'How to evolve a peaceful and prosperous society?' But my search for the complete truth continued. Then I happened to visit Bulgaria that same year.

At the end of a two-day state visit, I went to the famous Rila monastery. Founded in the tenth century by the followers of Bulgarian hermit saint Ivan Rilski, it is one of the most significant cultural centres of the nation and was completely rebuilt in the nineteenth century after it was destroyed in a fire. I was interested in the historical and spiritual aspects of the place considered to be holy by Bulgarians. I discussed the message from Tawang with the monks there. They supplied another part of the answer.

Their core message was that forgiveness is the foundation of a good life.

4. Giving Leads to Peace and Happiness

In 2004, I had a similar memorable experience at the birthplace of Swami Vivekananda. His ancestral home at 3 Gourmohan Mukherjee Street in north Calcutta was restored over five years and opened to the public amidst much fervour in October that year, and I was invited to inaugurate it.

Swamiji was born in that house in 1863. At that time it was surrounded by a garden and beyond that was a large open space. But in later years, owing to the city's growth, the approach road to the house narrowed down to a lane. The eighteenth-century building had been in a dilapidated state before the Ramakrishna Mission acquired and restored it as a memorial-cum-museum, along with a newly constructed cultural and research centre and textbook library on an adjacent plot.

I interacted with Swamiji's disciples on the occasion of the inauguration and spoke to them about my Tawang experience. They too felt that it was a beautiful message and added that the trait of giving adds to peace and happiness.

5. Good Deeds Result in Good Actions

I once visited the famous dargah of the Sufi saint Khwaja Moinuddin Chishti in Ajmer, Rajasthan. I participated in the Friday namaz there and interacted with a Sufi expert. He told me that the Almighty's creation, man, is challenged by a powerful force, Shaitan, the devil, who tempts man to perform evil deeds. Only good deeds lead to good thinking, and good thinking results in actions that radiate love as commanded by the Almighty.

~

When I was a boy of ten years, I would regularly witness the meetings of three people in my house: Pakshi Lakshmana Sastrigal, the head priest of the famous Rameswaram temple and a Vedic scholar; Reverend Father Bodel, who built the first church in Rameswaram island; and my father, who was an imam in the local mosque. All three of them would sit together and discuss the island's problems and come up with solutions. In addition, they built religious bridges with their compassion.

This memory always comes to my mind whenever I think of what kind of a world our youth need to strive to create. India has had a culture of integration of minds for thousands of years. What I wish to say is that we need to teach our youth to transcend the divides that exist in society. That is the only way for them to solve many of the problems plaguing our nation and the world.

SEVEN

FOR TEACHERS

I HAVE INTERACTED with more than 15 million schoolchildren across the length and breadth of the country. Wherever I went – be it Arunachal Pradesh, Nagaland, Madhya Pradesh, Gujarat, Karnataka, Jammu and Kashmir or any other part of India – the voice of the youth was unique and strong. They articulated their vision and were willing to work towards it. They all dream of living in a prosperous India, a happy India, a peaceful India and a safe India. Prosperity, happiness, peace and safety have to converge; only then will India truly be a developed nation. And the instruments who can help our children realize that vision are their teachers.

When I address any gathering of teachers and students, I realize that I am interacting with a small cross section of the community which lays the foundation of India's future. Teachers ignite the minds of students. According to government data, there are about 6.5 million schoolteachers in the country, and each one of them is a burning candle that lights many more. On an average, children spend about 25,000 hours in school during the twelve years of their primary and secondary education. Teachers can, therefore, have a lasting impact on the lives of students by becoming role models.

'WHAT CAN I DO FOR YOU?'

Every one of us has gone through the various phases of education. In each of those, I sometimes wonder, how do we react to human need? The child asks, 'What can you do for me?' The teenager says, 'I want to do it alone.' The young person proclaims, 'Let us do it together.' The leader offers, 'What can I do for you?'

Teachers, particularly principals or heads of educational institutes, bear the tremendous responsibility of transforming a child into a leader – from 'What can you do for me?' to 'What can I do for you?' This requires them to be visionaries, with a capability to inspire. Also, the principal has to ensure that teachers impart learning to children in such a way as to bring out the best in them. For this, he needs to be a good teacher himself.

I am sure that the best of creativity in students will emerge through the integrated influence of principals, teachers and parents.

MARVELS OF THE UNIVERSE

The human mind is a unique gift. You can enter what I like to call the 'marvels of the universe' only if you have curiosity and you are a thinking person. These should be your most important assets no matter what ups and downs you experience in life. Thinking is progress. Non-thinking is stagnation in the individual, the organization and the country. Thinking leads to action. Knowledge without action is useless and irrelevant. Knowledge with action brings prosperity.

Teachers should cultivate young minds to explore every aspect of human life. Look at the sky. We are not alone. The whole universe is friendly to us and conspires only to give the best to those who dream. As in the case of Subrahmanyan Chandrasekhar, whose mathematical treatment of stellar evolution yielded many of the best current theoretical models of the later evolutionary stages of massive stars and black holes. His quest had originated from a curiosity about why most stars shine and a few die. Today, using the Chandrasekhar limit, we can calculate how long the sun will shine.

Or take the example of Sir C.V. Raman, who looked at the sea and the sky and questioned why the sea should be blue. This led to the birth of the Raman Effect as he found that the blue of the sea was due to the molecular scattering of light and was not the result of the sky's reflection in water, as most people had imagined it to be. Or Albert Einstein, who asked how the universe was born. That led to the birth of the famous equation, $E=mc^2$, which led to a revolution in nuclear physics.

In India, an important event took place in the 1960s. Prof. Vikram Sarabhai gave India the vision of an indigenous space programme. He said that India should build its own rocket system and communication and remote sensing satellites, and conduct launches from its own centres. Today, India has all the capabilities that he dreamt of.

I would like to ask all the teachers of India if they can mould students to become noble-minded thinking persons like Sir C.V. Raman or Albert Einstein or Subrahmanyan Chandrasekhar or Vikram Sarabhai. I would like to tell them to look at the marvels of the universe and to realize that they have the power to create great thinkers.

EDUCATION WITH A GOOD VALUE SYSTEM

I remember the lectures of Reverend Father Kalathil of St Joseph's College, Tiruchirappalli, from the time I was a student there. He was the highest authority of the Jesuit institute. Every Monday he would take a class for an hour. He would talk about good human beings present and past and what made a good human being. He would talk about great personalities such as Gautam Buddha, Confucius, St Augustine, Califa Omar, Mahatma Gandhi, Albert Einstein and Abraham Lincoln. He would also tell us moral stories linked to our civilizational heritage. In the moral science class, Fr Kalathil would highlight how such great people were the products of parental care, teaching and the companionship of good books.

Even though I heard these lectures in the 1950s during my

college days, they continue to inspire me even six decades later. I believe it is essential that great teachers give lectures in schools and colleges once a week for an hour on India's civilizational heritage and place their students in a good value system. This will elevate the young minds to love the country and to love other human beings. It will also ensure that righteousness is instilled in each citizen at a young age.

CAPACITIES FOR NATION-BUILDING

The most important mission to which teachers can contribute is the creation of capacities for nation-building. In the education environment, what kind of human beings do we want to make of ourselves? What capacities do we want to give our children? If we want to give them certain capacities, we must ask: capacity for what? We want to give our children the capacity for contributing to economic development and nation-building. What kind of nation does India want to build?

Our vision for the nation is to transform India into a developed nation by 2020. There are five areas for simultaneous development: agriculture and food processing; education and health care; information and communication technology; infrastructure development, including networking of rivers; and self-reliance in critical technologies.

To achieve this mission, the capacities required in schools and in the students are: the capacity for research or inquiry; the capacity for creativity and innovation, particularly the creative transfer of knowledge; the capacity to use high technology, the capacity for entrepreneurial leadership and the capacity for moral leadership.

1. Research and Enquiry

The twenty-first century will be about the management of all the knowledge and information which we have available at our fingertips. We must give our children the skills with which they can wade through and make good use of it. Through technology, we today have the ability to truly become the lifelong learners that any sustained economic and political development requires.

2. Creativity and Innovation and the Creative Transfer of Knowledge

We can best teach ourselves by teaching others. The management of knowledge in the twenty-first century is beyond the capacity of individuals. The amount of information we must make sense of is overwhelming and has exceeded the capacity of individuals. The management of knowledge, therefore, must move out of the realm of the individual and into the realm of society. We must learn how to manage knowledge collectively. In other words, we must not only teach ourselves but teach others.

3. Use of High Technology

Every student in our schools should be able to use the latest technologies to aid his or her learning process. Schools should equip themselves with all the latest hardware, software, laboratory equipment and internet facilities, and provide an environment in which students are able to enhance their learning ability.

4. Entrepreneurial Leadership

Entrepreneurial leadership has three aspects. First, finding the problem and solving it in the context of development. Entrepreneurship starts with understanding our needs and realizing that, as human beings, we all have similar needs. It begins with wanting to help others as we help ourselves. Second, it is the willingness to take risks. Entrepreneurship means doing things differently, being bold in one's thinking, and that is always risky. We must teach our children how to take calculated risks for the sake of the larger gain. The third part is the disposition to do things right.

5. Moral Leadership

Moral leadership involves two things. First, it requires the ability to have compelling and powerful dreams, or visions of human betterment – a state in which human beings could be better off in the future than they are now. Second, where entrepreneurial leadership requires people to acquire the habit of doing things right, moral leadership requires a disposition to do the right thing and influence others also to do the right thing.

Educators today must exercise moral leadership themselves and also inculcate it in their students if our schools and educational institutions are to meet the challenges of the twenty-first century. They must develop a new vision for schools and schooling – a vision of an educational environment in which students can grow to be autonomous through the very act and process of learning.

Such an education for our children will provide the nation committed leaders who will transform India into a prosperous, peaceful, secure and happy nation.

If all these five attributes are inculcated in students by their teachers, parents and heads of the educational institutes where they study, they will have a burning desire to learn throughout their lives and set an example for others. In other words, they will be perfect learners. They will not only learn from the classroom but also from their environment. I firmly believe that every teacher's mission is to generate perfect learners.

Keeping this in mind, I have designed an eleven-point oath which I would like teachers all across India to follow:

1. First and foremost, I will love teaching. Teaching will be my soul.
2. I realize that I am responsible for shaping not just students

but ignited youths who are the most powerful resource under the earth, on the earth and above the earth. I will be fully committed to the great mission of teaching.

3. I will consider myself to be a great teacher, for I can lift what is average to the level of the best by way of my teaching.

4. All my actions in relation to my students will be deeds of kindness and affection. I will be to them a mother, sister, father or brother.

5. I will organize and conduct my life in such a way that it itself becomes a message for my students.

6. I will encourage my students to ask questions and develop the spirit of inquiry so that they blossom into creative, enlightened citizens.

7. I will treat all my students equally and will not support any differentiation on the basis of religion, community or language.

8. I will continuously build my teaching capacities so that I can impart quality education to my students.

9. I will take great pride in the success of my students.

10. I realize that by being a teacher I make an important contribution to all national development initiatives.

11. I will constantly endeavour to fill my mind with great thoughts and spread nobility in thinking and action.

EIGHT

FOR FARMERS

I COME FROM Tamil Nadu, the land of poet–saint Thiruvalluvar. Around 2,200 years ago he composed 1,330 couplets, together known as the Thirukkural. Of those, ten couplets were dedicated to the farming community and celebrated their profession. I grew up reading the Thirukkural and have deep respect for all the farmers of our nation. According to the latest census figures, there are as many as 120 million cultivators in India. Nearly 50 per cent of the country's workforce is in agriculture, which accounts for 13.7 per cent of the gross domestic product (GDP).

Let me share with you three experiences regarding the farming community in India which have showed to me how our farmers can make us a great nation. One story is from Bihar, another one from Tamil Nadu and the third from Gujarat.

DOUBLING PRODUCTIVITY, BIHAR

An experiment was conducted by the Technology Information, Forecasting and Assessment Council (TIFAC) team in Bihar, in RP Channel 5 and Majholi distributary, and later extended to Paliganj and five other distributaries on the request of farmers around the year 2000. The project was carried out by TIFAC in collaboration with a farmers' co-operative society, the Indian Agricultural Research Institute (IARI), and the agricultural university in Pusa, Bihar.

By using scientific methods of farming, such as soil characterization, matching the right seed to soil, planting in time, proper selection of fertilizers and pesticides, water management, and pre- and post-harvesting methodology, the productivity was more than doubled. The yield of paddy increased in these villages from 2 tonnes per hectare to 5.8 tonnes per hectare, and that of wheat from 0.9 tonne per hectare to 2.6 tonnes per hectare. At present, the paddy and wheat crops are spread over an area of more than 2,500 hectares and involve 3,000 farmers.

There is a need to replicate this success story in many other states.

PRECISION FARMING, TAMIL NADU

Precision farming or precision agriculture is a technology adopted in Tamil Nadu and involves doing the right thing in the right place at the right time. It has led to higher productivity, given farmers access to the market and made them entrepreneurs. It is a technique that helps to evaluate optimum sowing density, estimate fertilizer and other input needs, and predict crop yields more accurately. It helps avoid the application of unwanted practices to a crop without taking into consideration local soil and climate conditions. That is, it reduces labour, water, inputs such as fertilizers and pesticides, and ensures quality produce.

The Precision Farming Project was started in Tamil Nadu first in Dharmapuri district in 2004-05. It was implemented initially on 100 hectares, then 200 hectares in 2005-06 and 100 hectares in 2006-07. An amount of Rs 75,000 for the installation of drip irrigation and another of Rs 40,000 for crop production expenses was given to farmers. The first crop was taken up under the total guidance of scientists from the Tamil Nadu Agricultural University, while the subsequent five crops were taken up by the farmers in three years.

In the first year, farmers were unwilling to undertake this project because of their frustration due to the continuing drought in the area since 2002. But after seeing the success of the first 100 farmers and the high market rate for the produce obtained from this scheme, farmers started registering in large numbers for the second and third years.

During an Annual Farmers' Day meeting held in Salem, one of the precision farmers said during his speech, with tears in his eyes, that he had been able to see bundles of cash adding up to Rs 1,00,000 for the first time in his life because of the techniques he had followed in farming. This had attracted the attention of policymakers, bankers and insurance firms, whose frequent visits to the project site brought further economic relief to the farming community. A minimum of Rs 1,00,000 and a maximum of Rs 8,00,000 were the gross returns from one hectare, and this factor helped every farmer own a project. For instance, P.M. Chinnasamy, a farmer, produced 500 tonnes of brinjals from one hectare in fifteen months, and he became the resource farmer for hundreds of others who cultivated brinjal.

Precision farming is now spreading throughout the state as its practitioners have doubled the yield in forty-five crops compared to the national and state averages.

NINE PER CENT AGRICULTURE GROWTH, GUJARAT

In Gujarat, the agriculture ministry of the state government worked with the agriculture research wing of the Indian Institute of Management, Ahmedabad, and evolved a methodology to achieve higher productivity. Thanks to the initiative, the state has consistently maintained a growth rate of 9 per cent in agriculture, compared to 3 per cent at the national level. Moreover, this was despite the fact that Gujarat was impeded by factors like depletion of the water table, deterioration of soil and water conditions due to salinity ingress, irregularity of rainfall and recurrent drought in early 2000.

The story of Gujarat's agricultural turnaround is an eye-opener for the entire nation. There are many lessons to learn from it. The key ones among them are:

1. Providing quality seeds, fertilizers and pesticides at the right time to farmers.
2. Establishing an exclusive farmers' power grid, providing electricity at a low cost.
3. Desilting all water bodies before the monsoon and interconnecting them.
4. Setting up a government mechanism to buy excess produce through cooperative societies and market it internationally.

CONCLUSION

Over the years India has had many such success stories. The need now is to replicate them widely at the national level. India has to embark on a second Green Revolution, which will enable it to further increase its productivity in the agriculture sector. Such a revolution would see the farmer's domain enlarge from grain production to food processing and marketing through cooperatives. While doing so, utmost care would have to be taken of the various environment- and people-related aspects of development to ensure that it is sustainable. With that in mind, I have drafted this eight-point oath for farmers:

1. Agriculture is a noble mission. I love agriculture.
2. Land and water are our greatest resources. I will protect and preserve them.
3. I will use technology and good agricultural practices to improve productivity.
4. To make agriculture sustainable, I will resort to organic farming.

5. Children are our wealth. I will educate my children to enhance agricultural productivity and agro-processing.
6. I will convert agricultural waste into wealth in the form of biofuel and organic fertilizers.
7. I will work to create a symphony between agriculture, manufacturing and the services sector.
8. I will make Indian agriculture competitive nationally and internationally.

NINE

FOR SARPANCHES

I OFTEN SAY that the heart of India is its villages. There are roughly 5,83,000 of them in our country and around 70 per cent of our population resides there. Hence, villages have to play a crucial role in bringing about overall development in the country. A gram panchayat is the cornerstone of the local self-government system in India, with about 2,50,000 of them in existence. The sarpanch – the elected head of the panchayat – assumes a position of great significance. He or she is the focal point of contact between government officers and India's large village community. In some states such as Bihar, sarpanches have been empowered to look into various civil and criminal cases and given judicial power to punish and impose fines on those violating rules.

The next two decades are very important for India in transforming from a developing country to a developed one.

To achieve this vision, I would like to share with you some thoughts on possible missions.

PURA AND WOMEN

The one mission closest to my heart is the rural development initiative called Providing Urban Amenities in Rural Areas (PURA). It involves identifying rural clusters with growth potential and creating four types of connectivities for them:
1. Road, transportation and power connectivity.
2. Electronic connectivity in the form of reliable telecom, internet and IT services.
3. Knowledge connectivity in the form of good educational and training institutions.
4. Market connectivity that would enable farmers and others to get the best prices for their produce.

The government has decided to implement the PURA strategy in 5,000 rural clusters across the country in the next five years. But the success of this ambitious programme lies in the collaborative efforts and active participation of village leaders at the grass-roots levels. Moreover, women, with their inherent characteristics of compassion, patience, perseverance, honesty, sensitivity to social issues, hard work and constructive approach towards problem solving, will be able to play a vital role in realizing this mission. Such women, when empowered through the democratic process, can collectively produce spectacular results.

I am reminded of the Tamil Mahakavi, Subramania Bharati, who, in 1910, composed a poem about the women of India. A translation of it would read thus:

She walks with raised head,

With her eyes looking straight.

She has her principles.

Unafraid of anybody!

She has a lofty

And knowledge-based pride.

Such cultured women

Don't falter from the chosen path.

She drives ignorance away.

She welcomes the bliss of life

With learned mind.

This is the dharma

Of the emerging woman.

PURA AND SARPANCHES

Sarpanches can create awareness about PURA in rural communities so that they can come forward to contribute willingly to this development programme. The contribution could be in the form of:

1. Promoting and facilitating illiteracy eradication campaigns.
2. Explaining the usefulness of computers in village administration to provide transparent governance and economic advancement.
3. Forming village cooperatives for central procurement,

storage, preservation, processing and marketing of goods at attractive prices.

4. Working to provide better nutrition, sanitation facilities, safe drinking water and access to reproductive health care for healthy families and communities.

5. Fighting against social evils such as dowry, female foeticide, child marriage, child labour, domestic violence and ill-treatment and harassment of socially backward classes.

6. Encouraging women to attain economic independence through the formation of self-help groups with the help of microcredit and organizing various skill development programmes.

7. Facilitating the conservation of energy through the effective utilization of solar power, recycling waste for energy generation, and management of water through rainwater harvesting.

CONCLUSION

The process of transforming India into a developed nation has already commenced. All of us are working towards this cause in our own ways. We find many individual success stories of women generating income in the fields of agriculture, agro-processing, cottage industry, handicraft, sericulture, herbal farming and so on. Women are also leading movements against social evils with success. If such women toiling at the grass-roots level take it upon themselves to work persistently towards the singular goal of making India a developed nation by 2020, no one can stop us.

It is time for women sarpanches to become creative leaders. They can play a lead role in the implementation of PURA in their respective villages with the help of the central government, state governments, entrepreneurs and non-governmental organizations. This can be achieved by motivating the rural population and mobilizing their fullest support. This will be the key task of all women sarpanches. My ten-point oath for them is:

1. I believe that God has given me a unique opportunity to serve the people of my panchayat.
2. My mission is to develop the panchayat with people's participation.
3. I will ensure that I will be transparent and honest in all my dealings with people.
4. I will ensure that the people of my panchayat are free from gambling and drinking habits.
5. I will make my panchayat, including women, 100 per cent literate.
6. I will persuade the people of my panchayat to consider male and female children equal in all respects.
7. I will ensure the provision of sanitary facilities and safe drinking water in all dwellings in my panchayat.
8. I will ensure a clean panchayat and I realize that cleanliness starts at home.
9. I will activate all the water bodies in my panchayat.
10. I will make my panchayat a model panchayat.

TEN

FOR HEALTH CARE PROVIDERS

PROVIDING AFFORDABLE HEALTH care to everyone is a big concern for India. A great nation can only be shaped by healthy individuals. Hospitals, doctors and health care providers play a huge role in keeping the country in good health. As of 2015, there were about 9,50,000 allopathic doctors in India. In government hospitals, there is one doctor for 11,500 people. Every government hospital serves around 61,000 people, with one bed catering to 1,833 patients. India thus has a long way to go in improving its health care profile.

MY VISUALIZATION OF A TWENTY-FIRST-CENTURY HOSPITAL

In the total chain of medical care, the multi-speciality hospital is an important system. This is what I visualize a twenty-first-century hospital to be like:

1. The hospital gives every patient the confidence that he or she will be cured. The smiling doctors, nurses and the beautiful environment of the hospital building spread cheer and hope.
2. The patients are heard. All the doctors, nurses and paramedical staff believe it is their mission to alleviate the patients' pain. Wherever and whenever required, groups of specialists see the patients and swiftly arrive at treatment regimens.
3. The hospital consumes less electricity and water through the effective use of green building concepts.
4. The surroundings of the hospital are green, full of trees with seasonal flowers.
5. The patients' test reports are stored in a central database so that they are readily available and the patients or their relatives do not have to waste time and energy searching for them.
6. The design of the hospital is such that it enables quick movement of patients for timely treatment.
7. The hospital's equipment and services provide a clean and infection-free environment to the patients.
8. The patients consider that the hospital is the best place for them to stay and get treated.
9. The hospital is fully IT-enabled, leading to the patients' round-the-clock virtual connectivity with doctors, nurses and the hospital chief. The hospital is also connected to

other major hospitals in the country for consultation and advice.

10. The hospital conducts a daily medical conference to review the patients' unique problems and find workable solutions to them.

The planning and setting up of such patient-friendly hospitals for the twenty-first century, taking into account the needs of the future and systematically expanding the facilities, would require timely management of many aspects. The key to success is creative leadership at various levels.

ATTRIBUTES OF CREATIVE HEALTH CARE LEADERS

In my life I have seen three dreams which have taken shape first as a vision, then as a mission and finally as realization: the space programme of the Indian Space Research Organization (ISRO), the Agni programme of the Defence Research and Development Organization (DRDO) and Providing Urban Amenities in Rural Areas. Of course, these three programmes succeeded in the midst of many challenges and problems. What I have learnt about leadership from these three programmes is this:

1. A leader must have a vision.
2. A leader must have the passion to transform his or her vision into action.
3. A leader must be able to take unexplored paths.
4. A leader must know how to manage success and failure.
5. A leader must have the courage to take decisions.

6. A leader must have nobility in management.
7. Every action of the leader should be transparent.
8. A leader must work with integrity and succeed with integrity.

To make India's hospitals ready for the twenty-first century, ensuring good health of its billion-plus people, its creative leaders must strive to develop these qualities of creative leadership.

SIX VIRTUES HEALTH CARE PROVIDERS MUST HAVE

In November 2008, I delivered the fourteenth convocation address at Kathmandu University. After the ceremony, I visited Ka-Nying Shedrub Ling monastery in Boudhanath and met the chief monk, Chokyi Nyima Rinpoche, who is also a medical researcher. After the reception, he invited me to his study. He sprinted up five floors as if he were a young boy and I trudged behind him.

His chamber overlooked the Himalayas. Its air was spiritually charged. What surprised me was that his research students came from different parts of the world. He introduced me to his co-author, David R. Shlim, MD. Together they have written a book titled *Medicine and Compassion: A Tibetan Lama's Guidance for Caregivers*. The premise of the book is that most of us act as informal caregivers to our old, ill or disabled loved ones. We can hire professional caregivers but there still isn't enough help to go around.

Medicine and Compassion helps reconnect its readers with

the true spirit of their caregiving task. It uses the teachings of Buddhism to present practical tools to revitalize the caring spirit. It offers practical advice on dealing with people who are angry at their medical conditions or their care providers, people who are dying, or the families of those who are critically ill, and it provides inspiration to anyone who wishes to re-energize his patience, kindness and effectiveness.

Chokyi Nyima Rinpoche and I exchanged a few books. *Medicine and Compassion* was among the ones he gave me. I read it during my journey from Kathmandu to Delhi and liked it tremendously. The key takeaway from the book for me was the six important virtues a medical practitioner must possess. According to Rinpoche and Shlim, the six virtues are generosity, pure ethics, tolerance, perseverance, pure concentration and intelligence. These virtues will empower caregivers to deal with the needy with a humane heart. They should serve as guiding lights for medical practitioners, health care professionals, nurses and paramedical staff across the world.

THE POWER OF BELIEF

Another book that I have found inspiring is *The Biology of Belief: Unleashing the Power of Consciousness, Matter and Miracles*. Its author, Dr Bruce Lipton, who is a friend of mine, sent me a copy of the book and I found it to be a groundbreaking work in the field of new biology that will revolutionize our knowledge about thinking. Through the research of Dr Lipton and other scientists, stunning new discoveries have been made about the interaction between one's mind and body and the processes by which cells receive information. It shows that genes and DNA do not control our biology – that DNA is instead controlled by signals from outside the cell, including those from our thoughts. To put it simply, genes and DNA can be manipulated by our beliefs.

Taking that further, he argues that diseases and their cures have a basis in our thinking and its relationship with our cells. 'Doctors should not regard the power of belief as something inferior to the power of chemicals and scalpel. They should let go of the belief that the body and its parts are essentially stupid,' he says.

Mahatma Gandhi too says that thoughts shape one's destiny. Dr Lipton quotes him saying:

Your beliefs become your thoughts
Your thoughts become your words
Your words become your actions
Your actions become your habits
Your habits become your values
Your values become your destiny.

I would urge health care providers everywhere to read Dr Lipton's book and understand his message so that they can train their patients to use the power of their beliefs to recover from their illnesses.

MAN BECOMES WHAT HE THINKS ABOUT

In this context I would like to mention another book that I read and found inspiring. It was *The Miracle Man: An Inspiring True Story of the Human Spirit* by Morris Goodman. At the age of thirty-six in March 1981, Goodman was flying a plane when, without warning, its engine lost power. He tried to manoeuvre the plane back to the runway to make an emergency landing, but the aircraft flew through a low-hung set of power lines, crashed to the ground and flipped over. The accident left him paralysed, his spinal cord crushed and his first and second cervical vertebrae broken. He could not eat or drink or even breathe without support. All he could do was blink his eyes. Doctors, of course, said that he would be in this vegetative state for the rest of his life.

But that was what they thought, and it did not matter to Goodman. What mattered to him was what he himself thought. He pictured himself being normal again and walking out of the hospital. All he had to work with was his mind. But, he says in his book, once you have your mind, you can put things back together. After weeks of intense practice, Goodman was able to take his first breath without the use of a machine. Soon he began working with speech therapists until he was able to utter a single word: 'Mama'. A few months later he was moved to a rehabilitation centre where he began eating and working on learning to walk again. With physical therapy, he continued to work to improve his muscle strength and stamina until he could stand on his own. After several weeks, he was able to walk unassisted.

Doctors were at a loss. Goodman had set himself the goal of walking out of hospital by Christmas, and that is exactly what he did. His message for the world is, 'Man becomes what he thinks about.' I hope that health care providers keep such stories in mind when they treat patients and teach them to depend on the strength of their own thoughts, and not just medicines, for true healing.

CONCLUSION

I would like to conclude with two oaths for health care providers. The first for the nursing community:

1. I love my profession of nursing. It is a noble mission.
2. I realize that alleviating someone's pain is a great, godly mission.
3. I will treat all patients equally with kindness and care.
4. I will take special care of at least twenty rural patients.
5. I will be a lifelong learner in nursing.
6. I will follow the motto, 'Let my care remove your pain and bring smiles.'

And the second one for doctors:

1. I realize that, as a medical professional, I am carrying out God's mission.
2. I will always devote a part of my time to treating patients who cannot afford it.

3. I will never subject my patients to unnecessary diagnostic pain and will only recommend tests that are absolutely essential.
4. I will treat at least twenty rural patients every year at minimal cost by going to rural areas.
5. I will encourage the development of high-quality indigenous equipment and consumables by making use of them in all our diagnosis and treatment.
6. If I get into research in medical science, I will work in directed research for developing vaccines for HIV and finding a permanent cure for type I and type II diabetes.
7. I will follow the motto: 'Let my brain remove the pain of those who are suffering and bring smiles.'

ELEVEN

FOR CIVIL SERVANTS

AT THE BEST as well as the worst of times, it is India's civil service that keeps the nation going. There were as many as 50,000 civil servants in India as of 2010. They are the ones who look after the day-to-day administration of our vast country and keep it running smoothly even in unstable times.

I remember my experience in the mid-1990s of formulating India's Vision 2020 strategies. I was given the task of chairing the TIFAC. At its first meeting itself we decided that the council must evolve a plan to transform India into an economically developed nation by 2020. At a time when India's GDP was growing at 5 to 6 per cent per annum, we had to envisage a growth rate of at least 10 per cent per annum consistently for over ten years to realize the development vision. This really ignited the minds of all of us in the council.

The members of the TIFAC at that time included the principal secretary to the prime minister; nine secretaries to the Government of India; the chiefs of the Confederation of Indian Industry (CII), the Associated Chambers of Commerce and Industry of India (ASSOCHAM) and the Federation of Indian Chambers of Commerce and Industry (FICCI); the chairmen of IDBI, ICICI and IFCI banks; the chiefs of a number of public and private sector institutions; the vice chancellors of a number of universities; and scientists from the Department of Science and Technology (DST).

We debated and arrived at seventeen task teams with over 500 members who had consultations with over 5,000 people in various sectors of the economy. The committees worked for over two years, resulting in twenty-five reports which we presented to the then Prime Minister of India, Shri H.D. Deve Gowda, on 2 August 1996. This is an excellent example of how the representatives of different government departments and organizations – the best of minds that came from India's civil service – worked in an integrated way for national development.

Before I became the President of India, I interacted with many senior civil service officers during the Satellite Launch Vehicle (SLV) programme and later during the formulation and execution of the missile programme. Subsequently, I met hundreds of civil service officers during my address to civil service probationers at the Lal Bahadur Shastri National Academy of Administration, Mussoorie. During my presidency, civil servants in the making would come to Rashtrapati Bhavan and meet me before their final postings and take a five-point oath (which I will come to at the end of this chapter) from me. I continue to visit India's rural areas, where I suddenly come across familiar civil service officers who reminisce about their meetings with me at Mussoorie or Rashtrapati Bhavan and explain their current missions.

Here I would like to recall a poem which I had shared with our parliamentarians during my address to both Houses in 2005:

Where are we now, dear friends?
In the Mahasabha that shapes our history.
The call of the heartbeats of Indian people.
People ask us, people ask us:

Oh! Parliamentarians, the sculptors of Mother India,
Lead us into light, enrich our lives.
Your righteous toil is our guiding light,
If you work hard, we all can prosper.

Like King, so the people,
Nurture great thoughts, rise up in actions,
May righteous methods be your guide.
May you all prosper ever with Almighty's grace.

The destiny of our nation is as much in the hands of our civil servants as the parliamentarians. I would urge India's civil servants to understand and imbibe the message of this poem. If you work hard, we all can prosper.

INTERACTION IN MUSSOORIE

I visited Mussoorie in 2010 and interacted with the eighty-fifth foundation batch of newly inducted civil service officers and also addressed mid-career civil service trainees. I spoke to them about creative and innovative leadership and the evolution of a better world. After the session, some unique questions were raised by the participants. They highlight the opportunities and challenges in governance faced at the highest levels of the nation's bureaucracy.

I had asked the young officers to think of how they can be creative leaders who can pioneer great missions in life. After the lecture, one young lady officer got up and said, 'Dr Kalam, the bureaucracy is trained and known for maintaining the status quo. In this context, how can I be creative and innovative?' Another young officer said, 'Sir, right now, at the start of our service, we are all ethically upright and resolute for integrity. We all want to work hard and make a change. But in a decade's time, in spite of our surroundings, how can I continue to follow the same values with enthusiasm?'

To these questions I replied that young officers entering governance have to determine a long-term goal for which they will be remembered. This goal will inspire them at all times during their career and help them overcome all problems. I told them that the young bureaucrats of our nation have to remember that when they undertake difficult missions, there will be problems. But the problems should not become our captain; we have to defeat the problems and succeed.

Another young officer said, 'Dr Kalam, you said that we should work with integrity and succeed with integrity. But the political system and our seniors who are corrupt will definitely put pressure on us at some point to compromise on our ethical standards. How can we tackle this problem?' I thought about this problem, which is very pertinent and practical. I responded by recalling my own experience of working closely with politicians and administrators.

I have been Secretary in the DRDO, Scientific Advisor to the Raksha Mantri and Principal Scientific Advisor to the Government of India. In all these positions I was in charge of large missions with huge capital investments. But at no point did any leader or administrator approach me for favours. I told the young officers that they can establish a brand of integrity for themselves that will keep away all those who want them to compromise their ethics. Of course, this may mean facing some problems. But, eventually, the best in human beings will find a way to succeed.

GOVERNANCE FOR A BILLION

Ultimately, the job of a civil servant is to provide good governance to the nation. And governance is judged by how proactive and responsive to people's needs it is. It should help them lead a life which is morally upright, intellectually superior, and of high quality. This is possible through acquisition and enrichment of knowledge. How can these objectives be realized?

I feel we need to evolve a Societal Grid which comprises a Knowledge Grid, Health Grid and E-governance Grid that feed into the PURA Grid. The first will empower citizens with appropriate knowledge in a democratic way, thereby ensuring the growth of knowledge society. The second will ensure that the benefits of quality health care services reach the needy, thereby enhancing their quality of life and increasing individual productivity, which will in turn help the nation develop faster. The third will lead to transparency in government services and ensure that they reach all the people uniformly without any dilution of quantum or quality.

If these grids complement each other and infuse quality of services into the PURA Grid, which connects India's 6,00,000 villages, the villages will be empowered and we will have inclusive growth. Empowered villages ensure good and smart governance. I am confident that the establishment of the Societal Grid model is technologically possible and will help us achieve the goal of transforming India into a developed nation by 2020.

Shri Venkatesham Burra, IAS, was the collector of Medak district in Andhra Pradesh (now in Telangana) when I had a close interaction with him once as part of the Lead India 2020 training programme started by Prof. N.B. Sudershan Acharya. It is a programme that trains youth to become change agents to transform society. Its philosophy is that individual development leads to national development.

I asked Shri Burra a few questions about his work and the role of civil service officers in bringing about good governance. I would like to share his responses here:

APJ: How has the Lead India programme touched the lives of the youth in your district?

VB: When I was the collector of Medak district, I perceived that the Lead India programme could really grab the students' attention. I supported it in a big way and more than 50,000 students in the district were fortunate enough to receive the inputs of this great programme. It touched their very core and transformed their outlook on life. The change is evident in their interactions at home, in class or on the playground. It tapped into their hidden potential and improved their overall personality.

APJ: What was the biggest problem you faced and how did you solve it?

VB: Some people in the district suffer from extreme

deprivation. The extremely ill and physically challenged people find it difficult to earn their livelihood. Some of them starve. The mentally ill people who live on the streets are not treated with dignity. The problem was acute, and the usual government schemes and programmes did not address their issues at all. They were most neglected and uncared for.

I tried to attend to this problem by motivating the community and NGOs. A programme called Aasara was launched with the active participation of self-help groups. Its aim was to provide at least two meals a day to the needy, especially the old and terminally ill. In each village, a self-help group identified the needy and appointed an unemployed woman to serve two meals to them. All the material required for the programme was provided by the self-help groups and the locals.

Another programme called Ashraya was launched with active cooperation between the district administration and NGOs. Its intention was to create a life of dignity for the homeless mentally ill people. They were rescued from the streets and treated at government hospitals. They were restored to good health with the help of nutritious food and medical assistance and were then reunited with their families.

An organization called Social Accountability International based in New York awarded its SA8000 certificate – one of the world's first auditable social certifications for decent workplaces across all industrial sectors – to the Medak district administration in 2007 for its work. It thus became the first government agency in all of Asia to receive this certificate.

APJ: Do you have any suggestions for citizens to help them get better services?

VB: Citizens' awareness and their questioning attitude are very essential to a well-functioning democracy and administration. Every citizen of this country is legally entitled to a decent human life – with his or her basic needs of food, clothing and shelter taken care of. All of us together must want to make India one of the most developed and happiest nations in the world. The different pillars of our democracy should work together and not with the intention of outsmarting the other. It is our own people governing the country, not a foreign power ruling over us. Cooperation, participation and responsibility are thus the need of the hour.

MY EXPERIENCES WITH SOME CIVIL SERVICE OFFICERS

Friends, here I would like to recall my experiences with some civil service officers whom I consider to be examples of sterling leadership.

C.R. Krishnaswamy Rao

During the guided missile programme phase of 1982-83, when I was Director, Defence Research and Development Laboratory

(DRDL), Shri C.R. Krishnaswamy Rao Sahib was the cabinet secretary. Before the submission of a paper on the missile programme to the cabinet, there was a meeting with Shri R. Venkataraman, the then Raksha Mantri, where Rao Sahib and the three vice chiefs of the armed forces were present. At the high-level meeting, I was called to present the missile programme study report.

There was tremendous criticism from the armed forces that India had not successfully developed a single missile thus far, so the development and production of five missiles together could not be sanctioned. Dr V.S. Arunachalam, the then Scientific Advisor to the Raksha Mantri, and I explained that it would be a flagship programme. But the members were not convinced. That was when Shri Krishnaswamy Rao Sahib made a remark which still rings in my mind.

He said, 'Hon'ble Minister sir, I heard all the discussion. But I would like to convey one thing. The time has come for us to take a decision and explore a new path with courage. We should not be caught up in the past. At present we are seeing a committed and passionate leadership for the missile programme. I consider that all the missiles should be developed simultaneously in an integrated way.'

Based on this remark, Shri R. Venkataraman decided to call the programme the Integrated Guided Missile Programme. It was approved by the cabinet within two months of the meeting. I got the necessary funds, human resources and a new management structure, including the funds required for establishing certain key production facilities. Today, the orders to the production agency for the Prithvi, Agni, Akash and the BrahMos, the first-of-its-kind supersonic cruise missile, are valued at over Rs 93 trillion. Such is the power of a single vision of our bureaucratic leadership.

Prabhat Kumar

Friends, there are many turning points in a nation's life. They affect the trajectory of the nation's growth in different fields. I am going to share an incident that shows how a revolutionary change was brought about in internet usage in India.

I used to attend the monthly meetings of secretaries chaired by the cabinet secretary, Shri Prabhat Kumar, during 1998-99. I had keenly observed the proceedings of all the meetings and wondered why the government had an internet service provider (ISP) monopoly. One day, Shri Prabhat Kumar looked at me and said, 'Mr Kalam, I will form a team with you as the convener. Can you find a way of increasing internet use in India?'

'Internet density in our country is quite low,' I said, 'and we need a large number of service providers to enhance it. Of course, there is a national security issue involved due to internet communication traffic.'

Shri Kumar asked me whether the secretary in the Department of Telecommunications and I could meet and give our thoughts on this issue. The two of us formed a special committee chaired by Prof. M. Vidyasagar, the then director of the Centre for Artificial Intelligence and Robotics. He kept me informed of the committee's discussions. He told me that even though there was convergence on the issue of decentralization of ISP, there were concerns about data security.

I decided that the committee would make a presentation that addressed all the stakeholders' issues. I invited a few special participants, such as Prof. N. Balakrishnan of the Indian Institute of Science and the then chairman of the Railway Board since they were large internet users. I would hold the meetings after working hours so that all the members could attend.

The main objection raised by some of the participants related to the security angle. The specialists mentioned that there were technologies available using which we could maintain security. The other side argued that doing so would further lead to privacy issues. The counter-argument was that genuine users would have nothing to be afraid of; only those who wanted to misuse the internet would worry about the invasion of their privacy. This was debated for a substantial amount of time and finally a consensus emerged among all the participants in favour of opening up ISP to the private sector.

I informed Shri Prabhat Kumar of the recommendations of the committee. He got immediate approval from the cabinet for the recommendations to be put into action. The opening of ISP has enabled India to have more than 1,200 active service providers today. As of December 2011 they were servicing nearly 121 million users, the figure growing at a rate of about 20 per cent every year. Shri Prabhat Kumar should be remembered for his contribution not only by the millions of internet users but also the $100-billion IT industry.

Santhosh Babu

I met Dr Santhosh Babu, the then managing director of the Electronics Corporation of Tamil Nadu (ELCOT) and the chief executive officer of the Tamil Nadu e-Governance Agency (TNEGA), in 2009. I had gone to participate in the inauguration of the virtual contact centre and rural business hub at Hosur FOSTeRA (Fostering Technologies in Rural Areas), a rural business process outsourcing (BPO) conceptualized by him when he was the collector of Krishnagiri district. He and his team had enabled the training of school dropouts for employment in the rural BPOs that they had set up.

Dr Babu had become popular in the district, moreover, for achieving the target of near-zero dropouts. This he had done with the use of technology, community partnership and a detailed diagnosis of the problem. I was astonished to see the richness of data in the software he developed to track and monitor out-of-school children, the details of which can be accessed at www.back2school.in. The methodology he used brought out what the students and their families precisely needed, and the district administration arranged to provide those needs immediately.

For example, a girl named Nirmala had dropped out of school a number of times in spite of the best efforts of the district authorities. On detailed inquiry, it was found that her family needed a ration card, a house and a job for her mother. The district authorities then arranged to get them a ration card, a house as part of the Indira Awas Yojna, and a government job for the mother. Nirmala was admitted to the Kasturba Gandhi Balika Vidyalaya in class six. Once the collector had arranged to take care of the family's needs, she started going to school regularly.

The thing to note here is that Dr Babu and his team went into the details of why a child dropped out of school. Having established that, they removed the cause and facilitated the child's return to school. This led to a rapid reduction in the number of school dropouts. This example demonstrates that a committed and passionate civil service officer can definitely make a difference to societal well-being and overall happiness with the use of technology.

Swaran Singh

Dr Swaran Singh was the divisional commissioner of Jalandhar, Punjab, from September 2003 to August 2007. He and his wife, Amarjit Kaur, made use of the medium of telefilms to spread awareness about female foeticide, a serious problem in the state. Directed by Dr Singh and scripted by his wife, the two-hour film *Eh Tera Apmaan* tried to depict how the desire of a village woman to have a grandson brought misery to her family in the form of crime.

Alongside, Dr Singh took other measures at the ground level, such as organizing community celebrations to mark the birth of girls. All girls born on a particular day were given the same name by the district collector in some cases. Also, the killing of a female foetus was mourned by the community outside the home of the family or the clinic responsible for the abortion. There was no slogan shouting, just a peaceful, dignified shok sabha that embarrassed those who had eliminated the foetus illegally. It sent out a strong message to the rest of the community.

We can see how a committed civil servant can combat a widely prevalent social evil and bring about a big change in the attitude towards the girl child.

M.G.V.K. Bhanu

On 21 November 2011, I went to Jorhat, Assam, to address the World Tea Science Congress. There I addressed the administrative and police officers of Jorhat and Dibrugarh districts, a gathering organized by R.C. Jain, the district magistrate of Jorhat. I administered an oath titled 'I will work with integrity and succeed with integrity' to the participants. The pitch of the chorus went high when they said 'work with integrity' but it went down when they repeated 'succeed with integrity' after me.

The next day, though, I witnessed a pleasing scene at the World Tea Science Congress in the presence of the chief minister of Assam and the Jorhat administrative team. I saw in front of me the chairman of the Tea Board, M.G.V.K. Bhanu, an IAS officer, giving the introductory speech to the participants of the congress.

He said, 'Yesterday, Dr Kalam administered an oath to all the IAS and IPS officers, including myself. I would to like to assure you, Dr Kalam, that I have worked with integrity and succeeded with integrity during the last twenty-four years as an IAS officer in different parts of the state and the country. Now I am in the Tea Board. I was secretary to the chief minister of Assam. I would like to assure Dr Kalam that I have tried to create a brand of moral uprightness in all my tasks.'

He added that he had thought the whole night what he should be remembered for. He said he would like to be remembered for making India the largest producer and exporter of tea in the world.

I am very happy to share this unique experience. If every functionary of the Government of India has such a vision and mission, I am confident that we will get transformed into a developed nation well before 2020.

CONCLUSION

Maharshi Patanjali said in the *Yoga Sutra* some 2,200 years ago: 'When you are inspired by some great purpose, some extraordinary project, all your thoughts break their bounds. Your mind transcends limitations, your consciousness expands in every direction, and you find yourself in a new, great and wonderful world. Dormant forces, faculties and talents come alive, and you discover yourself to be a greater person by far than you ever dreamt yourself to be.' With these inspiring words in mind, let me conclude with my five-point oath for civil servants:

1. I will work towards 100 per cent literacy among the people of the region where I work and also ensure that no child drops out of school.
2. I will ensure that the status of women is enriched and work towards parity between girls and boys.
3. I will ensure that no one can lead me to the temptation of corruption.
4. During my tenure in any district, I will ensure that a minimum of one lakh trees are planted and maintained.
5. I will work towards the execution of at least five PURA complexes in the district where I'm posted and create employment opportunities for at least 25 per cent of the people through the creation of rural enterprises.

TWELVE

FOR THE JUDICIARY

ONLY A NATION that is just can hope to be known as a great nation. A robust judiciary plays an important role in laying the foundations of a great country by making its society just, equal and fair. At the same time, justice delayed is not only justice but also greatness denied. Unfortunately, in India, the phenomena of pendency of cases and inordinate delays in dispensing justice have plagued the judiciary for a long time, hampering national development. According to the data of the Ministry of Law and Justice, India's Supreme Court, high courts and district and subordinate courts together have more than 30 million pending cases, with nearly 10 per cent of them dragging on in courts for over a decade.

The reasons for this are many: inadequate number of courts and judicial officers (by one estimate, the Indian legal system suffers from a shortage of at least 70,000 judges); judicial officers not being fully equipped to tackle specialized cases; dilatory tactics deployed by litigants and their lawyers such as frequent adjournments and not filing documents on time; and, finally, the administrative staff of the courts.

A ROBUST JUDICIARY

The Indian judiciary should address these problems in a targeted way so that it becomes the driver of national development by delivering speedy justice. The backlog of cases can be cleared through human touch, age analysis of cases, an alternative dispute redressal mechanism, fast-track courts, e-judiciary, capacity enhancement and continuous training of judges, lawyers and the judicial staff. Cases that are similar from a legal point of view can be grouped and placed before a particular judge or bench for speedy disposal. For instance, a special mechanism can be set up to settle cases pertaining to each government department. Lawyers should proceed with their cases without seeking unnecessary adjournments, and there must be a limit to the number of adjournments permissible in a particular case.

The e-judiciary system will be the most crucial in reducing the agony of litigants. From the time a case is registered till it is disposed, the entire process must take place electronically. This will enable easy search, retrieval, grouping, information processing, judicial record processing and disposal of cases in a transparent manner. Transparency must start from home. Judges, lawyers, the support staff and litigants have all got to play a role and must be accountable for their actions.

The enormous responsibility of our nation's development rests on the shoulders of the courts. The judicial system must rise to the task with dynamism and innovativeness.

LAW AND ETHICS

It is also important to think of law not in isolation but in relation to the changing concerns of our time. During the last two hundred years, there has been considerable advancement in science and technology. Certain things which were considered possible in science have not happened, whereas certain other things not considered possible have become a reality. It would be tragic if our laws and ethics are unable to respond to the unending challenge of evolutionary and revolutionary changes in our society.

Given the rapidity of these developments and their impact on mankind and society, there is an urgent need to have a re-look at law, science and ethics in an integrated way. Scientists, technologists and legal experts need to work together and draw a roadmap for the changes which are needed in our legal system, taking into account technological progress to ensure a balanced social system.

Take the example of the human genome project, which I referred to earlier in the book. In relation to it, some questions which come to mind are: Who is the owner of the results of the project? Who should have access to personal genetic information, and how will it be used? Who owns and controls genetic information? How will genetic tests be evaluated and regulated for accuracy, reliability and utility? The other dimensions of law which need to be looked into are space laws and cyber laws.

The pursuit of science leads to an understanding of natural laws and it gives us the ability to apply them for practical purposes for human society. Similarly, the laws created for governing a society are legal in nature and help in maintaining order and harmony in society. But what is the law that keeps the practitioners of these different kinds of laws under control? Who creates them? I think this falls broadly under the term 'ethics'. The practice of ethics will demand much more than mere codes and procedures. Ultimately, it will require the transformation of individuals through proper education.

CONCLUSION

India was ruled by kings for thousands of years. Every ruler left behind a set of laws. Similarly, there have been many religions practised in India and they too had their own sets of laws. The British ruled us for over two hundred years and gave us the rule of law based on their political, religious and legal experiences. We have been following that for many decades now. Each system of laws has helped advance our society.

At present, India is going through a phenomenon wherein knowledge society is influencing information society, industrial society and agricultural society through innovation and value addition. Thanks to this, by the year 2020 India will become an economically developed nation. But the status of economic development alone has not resulted in a happy societal life in the real sense in many countries. This means that India, while working in mission mode towards economic development, should also build values and ethics based on our civilizational heritage into the evolution of our society. A legal system thus evolved, in sync with the different phases of India's development, will lead to a happy, prosperous and safe India.

I will conclude with an oath for India's budding lawyers and practitioners of the legal system:

1. I love my profession, the noble legal profession.
2. I will always work to establish the truth in all the cases I take up.
3. I will work towards making the legal system accessible to every citizen, irrespective of his or her economic or social status.
4. I will cooperate with the judicial system to ensure the speedy disposal of every case I take up.
5. I will use the provisions of the law to protect the dignity of every human life.
6. I will never make use of the provisions of the law to prove an innocent person guilty.
7. I will constantly use the provisions of the law to make the nation corruption- and terrorism-free.
8. I will never allow the law to be misused in such a way that

it hampers the promotion of human welfare and national development.

9. My nation is my life and I will use the legal knowledge to protect the sovereignty and integrity of my nation.

THIRTEEN

FOR POLITICAL LEADERS

FINALLY, I WOULD like to talk about the role of the political leadership in shaping a great nation. It is their decisions, their vision and their everyday actions that change the course of a country's destiny. There cannot be a great nation without an inspiring political leadership and so we need to think deeply about how to evolve creative leaders who can lead us by example on the pathways to greatness.

I recall my own experiences with some of the great political leaders that India has produced.

MY EXPERIENCES WITH THE GREATS

P.V. Narasimha Rao and Atal Bihari Vajpayee

It was 9 o'clock one night in May 1996. I got a call from the prime minister's house and was told to meet P.V. Narasimha

Rao immediately. I met him just two days before the results of the general election were declared. He told me, 'Kalam, be ready with your team for a nuclear test. I am going to Tirupati. Wait for my authorization to go ahead with the test. DRDO–DAE (Department of Atomic Energy) teams must be ready for action.' The journey to the temple town was to pray for success in the election.

As it turned out, the result was quite different from what he had anticipated. I was busy at the Chandipur missile range in Orissa. I got a call saying that I must immediately see the prime minister designate, Atal Bihari Vajpayee, with the outgoing PM. I was struck by the fact that Rao was asking me to brief Vajpayee on the nuclear programme so that a smooth takeover of this very important activity could take place. This incident reveals the maturity and professional excellence of a patriotic statesman who believed that the nation is bigger than the political system.

Of course, after taking over as prime minister in 1998, the first task given by Vajpayee to me was to conduct the nuclear test at the earliest. Both these leaders had the courage to take difficult decisions boldly, even though the consequences of such decisions had great national and international significance.

Indira Gandhi and Biju Patnaik

Prime Minister Indira Gandhi had sanctioned the Integrated Guided Missile Development Programme in 1983. I was Director, DRDL, Hyderabad, in 1984 when she came there to review the programme. As we were presenting its progress to Mrs Gandhi, her eyes fell on a world map in the conference hall. She asked us to stop the presentation and said, 'Kalam, look at the map, look at the distance in the eastern side of the map. When will the laboratory launch a missile which will be capable of reaching that spot (which was 5,000 km away from Indian territory)?'

This reminds me of another incident that took place in 1993 when we at the DRDO were looking for a suitable location to launch test missiles. Our efforts to conduct the tests in the desert stretches in the western part of India could not take off due to range safety and geopolitical concerns. To overcome this, we were looking for an uninhabited island on the eastern coast. On a hydrographic map supplied by the navy, we saw a few islands in the Bay of Bengal off Dhamra in Orissa. Our range team consisting of Dr S.K. Salwan and Dr V.K. Saraswat hired a boat from Dhamra and went in search of the islands. On the map these islands were marked as 'Long Wheeler', 'Coconut Wheeler' and 'Small Wheeler'. The team carried a directional compass and proceeded on the journey. But they lost their way and could not locate the Wheeler islands.

Fortunately, they came across a few fishing boats and asked them for directions. The fishermen did not know about the Wheeler islands but said there was one called Chandrachood. The scientists thought this could be one of the Wheeler islands. They took approximate directions to Chandrachood island from the fishermen and proceeded in that direction. With this help the team managed to reach Chandrachood island, which was later confirmed as Small Wheeler. It had the width and length required for our operations.

The next step was to get authorization from the Orissa government for use of the islands. We went through the state bureaucracy and finally had to seek a political decision from Chief Minister Biju Patnaik. There were indications from his office that our request would be turned down for several reasons. Nevertheless, a meeting with the chief minister was arranged.

When we reached his office, the file was placed in front of him. 'Kalam,' he said, 'I have decided to give all five islands at no cost to you (DRDO), but I will sign the file only when you give me a promise.'

I wondered what this powerful leader wanted from me.

He held my hand and continued, 'I have an invitation to visit China. But I will visit only when you promise that you will make a missile that will reach China.'

'Sir, we will definitely work towards it,' I said and the chief minister signed the file.

It was the vision of great leaders like Indira Gandhi and Biju Patnaik that drove our scientists to successfully launch the nuclear-capable Agni V, with a range of 5,000 km, two decades later in 2012.

A CALL TO PARLIAMENTARIANS

When I look at India's parliamentarians, I see in them the promise of Narasimha Rao and Atal Bihari Vajpayee, Indira Gandhi and Biju Patnaik – of Dr Rajendra Prasad, Pandit

Jawaharlal Nehru, Netaji Subhas Chandra Bose, Sardar Vallabhbhai Patel, Dr Babasaheb Ambedkar, Maulana Abul Kalam Azad and Mahatma Gandhi. They were India's visionary leaders. My question to the parliamentarians of today is: Can you also become visionary leaders, putting the nation before yourself? Can you also be counted among the great leaders India has produced? Yes, you can.

The vision of independent India's original great leaders has held the country in good stead for the past seven decades. India can rightly be proud of its many achievements in the economic, social and political fields. But we cannot afford to rest on our laurels. The leadership of today's parliamentarians, legislators and political leaders can shape India's destiny for several more decades to come. A great responsibility rests on their shoulders.

The political leadership must instil confidence in our people by formulating and implementing new national missions, targeting specific time-bound goals. We need to face up to several challenges: strengthening internal security to cope with global terrorism and new forms of internal law and order problems; the widening of economic disparities; the rapid depletion of global fossil fuel reserves; planning for the penetration of communication systems and computers; and providing safe drinking water, uninterrupted electricity, health care and shelter to a billion people.

These are national issues which our political leaders need to address going beyond party lines and ideologies. Parliament is the pivotal institution of any democracy and so it is parliamentarians who need to take the lead in tackling them. The mission for them could be the evolution of a vision for the nation. It is up to them to give a prosperous, peaceful and secure future to the people. The parliamentarians' role, therefore, assumes tremendous significance and it is essential that each one of the members of Parliament lives up to the aspirations and ideals for which he or she has been elected. In every parliamentarian, our youth should see great leaders who can be their role models and who will bring about a dynamic change in politics and society.

Here I would like to address India's honourable members of Parliament directly and say that only you can bring smiles on the faces of a billion people by enacting appropriate policies and laws and facilitating societal transformation. Your names are waiting to be written in the important pages of the history of India. Transform India into a developed nation and the glory could be yours. Show the world the maturity of your politics and how you can utilize it for the sustained development of our nation. Strive to build an India that is vibrant, vigilant, safe and secular. I am sure that this is well within your capabilities and you can achieve it if you really want to.

CONCLUSION

I recall an incident that took place on 19 January 2011. I was in Amravati, Maharashtra, to attend a programme organized by the Satpuda Shikshan Prasarak Mandal. As part of it, I addressed one lakh youth on the subject 'I Am Unique' in the presence of many political and social development leaders, teachers and educationists. After I finished my talk, among several other questions that came up, an interesting one was posed by a young boy.

He introduced himself as a class ten student from Harali village. 'Sir,' he asked, 'our media and my friends always say that China is progressing well economically and at a faster pace than India. Please tell me, sir, why India cannot grow faster and tell us what youngsters like me can do to make sure that happens?'

There was a thunderous ovation in response to this boy's question. A crowd of one lakh youth needed an answer from me. My friends on the dais too looked at me expectantly. Reflecting for a brief moment, I asked the boy his name.

'Vineet,' he said.

'Vineet,' I said, 'you have a powerful mind and you also love your nation. My answer for you is that it is true that China's economic progress is quite different from India's. But, unlike China, India is a democracy with a parliamentary system. Its leaders are elected by its people. Democracy comes with its pulls and pressures. But we must keep flying. The leadership has to strive to eliminate the delay associated with democracy. What I want to ask all the youth assembled here, dear young friends, is that suppose I give you a choice of the two systems – one with a full democracy and a high pace of development, and the other a political system like China's – which one would you prefer?'

When I asked them to indicate their preference with a show of hands, 99 per cent of the youth raised their hands and said that they wanted to live in a democracy with a faster rate of growth. The message was loud and clear: 'The youth definitely want our democracy to be reinvented with faster growth.'

I call upon our political leaders to reinvent our democracy and alter the course of the nation's destiny. I will conclude with an oath for our parliamentarians:

1. I realize my responsibilities because my constituency has elected me to lead them.

2. I realize that leading my people means I have to bring prosperity and peace in my constituency.

3. My main goals for my constituency would be: 100 per cent literacy, activating all water bodies, ensuring all primary health care centres start functioning, and, above all, a peaceful constituency.

4. I will always ask, 'What can I give?' This will indeed make me serve with humility.

5. I will work with integrity and succeed with integrity.

6. I will ensure that my constituency has a green environment by planting 2 million trees.

7. Let my brain remove pain.

8. My national flag flies in my heart and I will bring glory to my nation.

SECTION III

FINAL THOUGHTS

FOURTEEN

THE IMPORTANCE OF LEADERSHIP

I URGE ALL sections of our society to imbibe these oaths and put them into practice in everyday life. We will then have creative leaders in all walks of life who will guide our nation on the pathways to greatness. I cannot emphasize enough the importance of leadership because it is often their singular vision that shapes the destiny of a great nation. Let us look at some examples from India's history of how a few leaders transformed the fields they worked in.

THE FREEDOM MOVEMENT

India's freedom movement created a number of visionary, devoted and passionate leaders in multiple fields such as politics, spirituality, literature, fine arts, judiciary, science and industry. In the field of politics, Lokmanya Bal Gangadhar Tilak proclaimed in the 1880s the fiery words, 'Swaraj is my birthright and I shall have it,' and breathed new life into our struggle for independence. Jamsetji Tata set up the steel industry in India even though the colonial rulers were not favourably disposed to the idea and also sowed the seeds for the creation of the Indian Institute of Science in Bangalore. In the field of education, Sir Syed Ahmad Khan founded the Aligarh Muslim University in 1875, while Pandit Madan Mohan Malaviya established the Banaras Hindu University in 1916. Acharya P.C. Ray, a professor of chemistry at Calcutta University, was a pioneer in the field of pharmaceuticals in India.

Prof. Subrahmanyan Chandrasekhar, an Indian-American astrophysicist who was awarded the Nobel Prize for physics in 1983, noted in his autobiography how in the 1920s there were five great scientists of international repute working in India: C.V. Raman, J.C. Bose, Srinivasa Ramanujan, S.N. Bose and Meghnad Saha. Chandrasekhar believed that this was not a happy coincidence but they were driven to prove that Indian minds could match the best in the world. He also said that the need for self-expression and assertion, whether in politics or science, was a dominant motive for the younger generation and was reflected in the national movement.

In the field of literature, Rabindranath Tagore won the Nobel Prize in 1913. At a time when the vision of freedom for India seemed remote, Tagore inspired his countrymen towards independence with conviction and passion through his writing:

Where the mind is without fear and the head is held high...
Into that heaven of freedom, my Father, let my country awake.

During the same time, the poems of the great Tamil poet, nationalist and revolutionary, Subramania Bharati, envisioned a great India, where women would be free and education would be widespread. In 1910, he wrote a poem – a song of freedom – which said: 'Let us celebrate, our blissful freedom has already arrived.' In the field of music, it was a unique phenomenon to see the trinity of Tyagaraja, Muthuswami Dikshitar and Syama Sastri enriching Carnatic music in the eighteenth century. Pandit Vishnu Narayan brought about a renaissance in Hindustani classical music.

India witnessed the rise of several inspiring women leaders too at this time. Bhima Bai Holkar, Rani Chennamma of Kittur, Rani Lakshmibai of Jhansi, Begum Hazrat Mahal of Avadh in the nineteenth century and Sarojini Naidu, Kasturba Gandhi and Annie Besant in the twentieth century are names which are remembered with reverence even today for their contributions on the battlefield and in the political field.

Finally, many great leaders such as Pandit Jawaharlal Nehru, Subhas Chandra Bose, Sardar Vallabhbhai Patel, Maulana Abul Kalam Azad, Dr Rajendra Prasad and C. Rajagopalachari, under the inspirational leadership of Mahatma Gandhi, spearheaded the independence movement and won for India her hard-fought freedom.

VIKRAM SARABHAI: A GREAT VISIONARY

India has seen several great leaders in different fields after independence too and I have been fortunate enough to work with a few of them. The one I remember with great admiration is Dr Vikram Sarabhai. While working closely with him for seven years at ISRO, I saw the dawn of India's space programme in his famous one-page statement in 1970.

It stated: 'India with her mighty scientific knowledge and powerhouse of young should build her own huge rocket systems (satellite launch vehicles) and also build her own communication, remote sensing and meteorological spacecraft and launch from her own soil to enrich the Indian life in satellite communication, remote sensing and meteorology. The projects selected in space programme are designed to meet the societal needs.'

It was a tremendous learning experience for me to work with this great leader who shaped India's future. If I look back at his vision statement now, over four decades later, I am overwhelmed by the results. Today, India can build any type of satellite launch vehicle, any type of spacecraft and launch them from Indian soil. India has also launched Chandrayaan and Mangalyaan and is now preparing for manned missions to other planets. India has proved that through space science and technology we can provide effective communication, resource mapping, disaster predication and disaster management systems.

Dr Sarabhai charted a path for India that no one had imagined before him. I particularly recall one incident that exemplifies this characteristic in him. It was in the early 1960s that he and his team had located a place technically most suited for space research after considering many alternatives. Thumba in Kerala was selected as it was near the magnetic equator, ideal for ionospheric and electrojet research in the upper atmosphere.

The major challenge for Dr Sarabhai was to get a place in a specific area. As was the norm, he approached the Kerala administration first. After seeing the profile of the land and the sea coast, the view expressed was that thousands of fishing folk lived there. The place had an ancient church, a bishop's house and a school. Hence, the administration felt that it would be very difficult to give away this land. They were willing to provide land in an alternative area instead. However, there was a suggestion to approach the only person who could advise and help.

That was Reverend Father Peter Bernard Pereira, who was the bishop of the region. Dr Sarabhai approached him on a Saturday evening, I still remember. The meeting between the two turned out to be historical. Many of us witnessed the event.

'Oh Vikram, you are asking for my children's abode, my abode and God's abode,' the bishop exclaimed. 'How is it possible?'

Both men had one thing in common. They could smile even in the most difficult situations. The bishop asked Dr Sarabhai to come to church on Sunday morning at 9 a.m. Dr Sarabhai and his team did so. When they reached the church, a prayer was in session. After it was over, the bishop invited Dr Sarabhai to come to the dais.

'Dear children, here is a scientist, Dr Vikram Sarabhai,' he said to his audience. 'What do sciences do? All of us experience, including this church, the light from electricity. I am able to talk to you through the mike – which is made possible by technology. The diagnosis and treatment of patients by doctors comes from the medical sciences. Science, through technology, enhances the comfort and quality of human life. What do I do as a preacher? I pray for you, for your well-being, for your peace. In short, what Vikram and I do is the same. Both science and spirituality seek the Almighty's blessings for human prosperity in body and mind. Dear children, Vikram says he would build, within a year, near the sea coast, alternative facilities for the ones we have now. Dear children, can we give your abode, can we give my abode, can we give God's abode for a great scientific mission?'

There was pin-drop silence. Then all the people gathered in the church got up and said 'Amen'.

In place of the church we set up our design centre, where we started rocket assembly. The bishop's house became our scientists' workplace. That was where we set up the Thumba Equatorial Rocket Launching Station, which later led to the establishment of the Vikram Sarabhai Space Centre. The space-related activities started there resulted in the proliferation of multiple space centres throughout the country. The church has now become an important centre of learning where thousands of people learn about the dynamic history of India's space programme and about the great minds of a scientist and a spiritual leader. Of course, the citizens of Thumba got a new school and a place of worship in an alternative location.

When I think of this event, I see how enlightened spiritual

and scientific leaders can converge for the good of human life. Of course, the birth of the Thumba Equatorial Rocket Launching Station and then the Vikram Sarabhai Space Centre gave the country the capability of launch vehicles, spacecraft and space applications that have accelerated social and economic development in India to unprecedented levels.

Today, neither Dr Sarabhai nor Father Pereira is with us, but they remind me of these lines from the Bhagavad Gita: 'See the flower – how generously it distributes perfume and honey. It gives to all, gives freely of its love. When its work is done, it falls away quietly. Try to be like the flower, unassuming despite all its qualities.' What a beautiful message to humanity on the purpose of life.

PROF. SATISH DHAWAN: MANAGING SUCCESS AND FAILURE

Three decades ago, while I was working at ISRO, I received the best education which I wouldn't get from any university. I was given a task by Prof. Satish Dhawan, the then chairman of ISRO, to develop the first satellite launch vehicle, SLV-3, to put the Rohini satellite in orbit. This was one of the largest high-technology space programmes undertaken at the time. The whole space technology community was geared up for this task. Thousands of scientists, engineers and technicians worked round the clock, resulting in the first SLV-3 launch on 10 August 1979.

SLV-3 took off in the early hours and we got through the first stage smoothly. Even though all rockets and systems worked, the mission could not achieve its objectives, as the control system in the second stage malfunctioned. Instead of being placed in the orbit, the Rohini satellite went into the Bay of Bengal. The mission was a failure.

There was a press conference at Sriharikota, Andhra Pradesh, after the event. Prof. Dhawan took me to it. And there he announced that he took the responsibility for the mission's failure even though I was the project director and the mission director. The next year, when we launched SLV-3 on 18 July 1980, successfully injecting the Rohini satellite into orbit, there was a press conference once again. This time around, Prof. Dhawan put me at the forefront to share the success story with the press.

What we learn from this event is that a true leader always gives credit for success to those who worked for it but takes the responsibility for failure. This is leadership. The scientific community in India has had the good fortune of working with leaders of such calibre, and that has resulted in its many accomplishments.

This is an important lesson for all the youth who are aspiring to be tomorrow's leaders. The great lesson we learn is that true leaders in any field – political, administrative, scientific, education, industry, judiciary or any other sphere of human activity – should have the capacity for creative leadership and the courage to absorb failures and to give the credit for successes to their team members.

DR BRAHM PRAKASH: NOBILITY IN MANAGEMENT

The next leader I would like to talk about is Dr Brahm Prakash, a metallurgist known for his work with nuclear materials. When I was the project director of the SLV-3 programme, Dr Prakash was the director of the Vikram Sarabhai Space Centre. He took hundreds of decisions for the growth of space science and technology in India. One of his most important decisions that I will always cherish was that once a programme such as the SLV-3 was sanctioned, the multiple laboratories of the Vikram Sarabhai Space Centre and also the multiple centres of ISRO, including the Space Department, had to work together as a team to realize the stated goals of the programme. During 1973–80, particularly, there was a tremendous financial crunch and competing requirements from many small projects. But he arranged for all scientific and technological work to be focused on the SLV-3 and its satellite.

When I say that Dr Prakash is famous for the evolution of nobility in management, I would like to give a few instances. He enabled, for the first time, the evolution of a comprehensive management plan for the SLV-3 programme towards the mission of putting the Rohini satellite in orbit. After my task team had prepared the SLV-3 management plan, in a period of three months he arranged nearly fifteen brainstorming meetings of the Space Scientific Committee. After many rounds of discussion, this management plan was signed by Dr Prakash and became the guiding light for the work of the whole organization. This was also the beginning of the conversion of the national vision into mission mode programmes.

During the evolution of the management plan, I saw the emergence of different and divergent views. Several people were afraid of losing their individuality to the cause of the main mission and their tempers would rise during the meetings. But I also saw Dr Prakash smiling through it all. People's anger, fears and prejudices all disappeared in the presence of his nobility in thinking.

Today, the space programme, scientific experiments and launch missions are taking place at ISRO centres in a cohesive and cooperative manner. I learnt from this great, mighty soul that before starting any programme it is essential to put in place a project management plan, complete with details of how to steer it during its different phases, how to foresee the possible critical paths and their solutions – time, performance and schedule being the key factors. I thank him for evolving the concept of management with nobility.

E. SREEDHARAN: PASSION TO REALIZE THE VISION

One of the more recent leaders India has witnessed is 'Metro Man' E. Sreedharan. He is an outstanding example of how one person's passion to realize a vision can transform the lives of millions of people. First with the Konkan Railway and then the Delhi Metro, he changed the face of public transport in India.

Under his stewardship, the Konkan Railway project was executed in seven years despite great difficulties. It had ninety-three tunnels along a length of 82 km and involved tunnelling through soft soil. It covered 760 km and had over 150 bridges. That a public sector project could be completed without significant cost and time overruns was considered a great and rare achievement.

He was then made the managing director of the Delhi Metro Rail Corporation and, under his leadership, all the scheduled sections were completed by their target date or before, and within their respective budgets. He was particularly known for isolating his projects from political pressures and influences and winning political commitments for fast execution. It was his passion and vision that gave India its first public transport system of truly international standards. The Delhi Metro is now the twelfth largest metro system in the world, with a total length of more than 200 km, consisting of over 150 stations, and serving around 2.6 million commuters daily. Not only that, it has also been certified by the United Nations as the first metro rail and rail-based system in the world to get carbon credits for reducing greenhouse gas emissions and helping reduce pollution levels in the city.

Sreedharan's stint in the Delhi Metro was so successful and crucial to India that France awarded him the Chevalier de la Légion d'honneur (Knight of the Legion of Honour) in 2005 and the Indian government awarded him the Padma Vibhushan, the country's second highest civilian honour, in 2008. He had announced that he would retire by the end of 2005, but his tenure was further extended to oversee the completion of the second phase of Delhi Metro. After sixteen years of service with the Delhi Metro, he retired from service on 31 December 2011. He has had little rest in retirement, though, and has been roped in as an advisor for metro systems in Kochi, Lucknow, Jaipur, Visakhapatnam and Vijayawada.

GLOBAL LEADERSHIP

It is leaders like these who make and will continue to make India great. But, I often say, having a small aim is a crime. And so we must not be content with creating a great nation. There is, after all, only one world that the whole of mankind shares and our ultimate goal must be to create a great planet.

I recall here the dreams of the visionary spiritual leader, Sri Aurobindo. The first of these was a revolutionary movement to create a free and united India. This was realized on 15 August 1947. The second was the resurgence and liberation of the people of Asia and India's return to her great role in the progress of human civilization. His third dream was for India to play a key role in the founding of a global union for a just, bright and noble life for all of mankind.

India should join hands with the other great nations of the world to realize this dream. It should be a global partnership to create an inclusive, just, prosperous and strong world order. I believe there are three missions which will be key:

1. *An Enlightened Society:* For evolving citizens with value system, leading to a prosperous and peaceful world.
2. *Energy Independence:* For realizing the dream of a clean planet Earth that most of us share.

3. *World Knowledge Platform:* For synergizing the core competences of all the nations of the world to come up with solutions to critical issues like water scarcity, quality health care for all and capacity building in all crucial fields.

Our movement for true freedom and independence is still incomplete; our story is still unfolding. The global environment is dangerous, and India's freedom – won by suffering and sacrifice – has to be alertly guarded, strengthened and expanded. Freedom and independence must be our continuing quest, and in such a manner as to accelerate our evolution as a free and safe nation through bold and swift actions.

India is a fairly young nation and the largest democracy in the world. Within this short time, and given the constraints of our population and political system, we have accomplished a significant degree of national development while facing many trials and tribulations – some in the form of nature's fury, some in the form of wars and cross-border terrorism. In spite of these happenings, we have been able to achieve self-reliance in meeting the food requirements of our billion-plus people through the Green Revolution. We have managed to increase the average lifespan with better primary health care centres in rural India. Our industrial base has been broadened. Science and technology have been given a new thrust with considerable successes in the fields of information and communication technology, space, atomic energy and defence research.

But no nation can exist in isolation. Global connectivity is real and vital. Ensuring global peace and the development of all of mankind will create a safer world that all nations of the world will benefit from. The major challenges facing humanity are removal of poverty, ensuring energy and drinking water availability and environmental protection. Many nations are suffering from unrelenting cross-border terrorism and insurgencies. These are not problems that are restricted to one country or region alone but have emerged as global threats to peace and harmony.

The world over, poverty, illiteracy and unemployment are driving forward the forces of anger and violence. These forces link themselves to historical enmity, tyranny, injustice, ethnic issues and religious fundamentalism, resulting in an outburst of terrorism worldwide. We need to address the root causes of such phenomena – poverty, illiteracy and unemployment – to create a peaceful and harmonious world.

The stability of any society is a vital factor that determines peace. It revolves around providing people's basic needs such as food, clothing, shelter and safety and security. People who are economically or socially in the lower strata are vulnerable to exploitation by those in the higher. One way to curb the exploitation is to narrow this divide. Visionary policies should emerge at the global level to eradicate poverty and to ensure that the basic needs of every human being are met, thereby reducing the gap between the haves and the have-nots.

How are we going to achieve this? The nations of the world need to take a consortium approach to ensure a global sharing of resources to address these issues for coexistence and co-development. Globally, there will be crises in the coming decades – for energy, clean water and environmental protection. Many nations have to come together to evolve visions to solve these so that generations of our youth globally live peacefully. When there is a vision for a nation with focused missions, problems like terrorism and violence will be eliminated.

FIFTEEN

THE IMPORTANCE OF PURA

IF I WERE to offer one focused mission that would go a long way in creating a great planet for all, it would be the grass-roots mission close to my heart – PURA. I have touched upon it earlier in this book, but I would like to discuss it in detail here as I feel it is the need of the hour and can bring inclusive growth and integrated development in all the nations of the world, starting with India.

PURA PROFILE

The development of 6,00,000 villages is vital for transforming India into an economically developed nation. It means that:

1. The villages must be connected within themselves and with main towns and metros by good roads and railway lines. They must have other infrastructure like schools, colleges,

hospitals and amenities for the local population and visitors. Let us call this physical connectivity.

2. In the emerging knowledge era, native knowledge has to be preserved and enhanced with the latest tools of technology, training and research. The villages have to have access to good education from the best teachers wherever they are, must have the benefit of good medical treatment, and must have latest information on their pursuits like agriculture, fishery, horticulture and food processing. That means they have to have electronic connectivity.

3. Once the physical and electronic connectivities are enabled, knowledge connectivity is enabled. That can facilitate an increase in productivity, the utilization of spare time, spreading of awareness about health welfare, ensuring a market for products, and an increase in quality conscience and transparency.

4. Once the three connectivities are ensured, they facilitate better earning capacity.

Thus, with PURA as a mission, we can transform villages into prosperous knowledge centres, and villagers into entrepreneurs. The number of PURA complexes needed for the whole of India is estimated to be 7,000, covering the 6,00,000 villages where around 750 million people live. Similarly, about 30,000 PURA complexes would be required to convert the 3 billion rural population of the world into a vibrant economic zone and bring sustainable development to rural areas.

The Government of India is already moving ahead with the

implementation of PURA at the national level across several districts of India with an outlay of Rs 1,500 crore under a public–private partnership model. There are several operational PURAs in India initiated by many educational and health care institutions and the industry: the Periyar PURA in Tamil Nadu, the Loni Warana Valley PURA in Maharashtra and the Chitrakoot PURA in Madhya Pradesh.

PURA ACTIVATED

Now let me present PURA Activated, a platform which is a unique enterprise-driven model of sustainable development. The essence of PURA Activated is the belief that the PURA enterprises of the next generation need to think of themselves as providers of more than mere livelihood. PURA Activated envisages the overall, integrated development of the rural population in the PURA complex. Moreover, it has the vision of sustainable socio-business models which act as a vertically integrated network of multiple entrepreneurs who share synergies and provide for value addition to each other, leading to the overall benefit of all stakeholders.

PURA Activated has two kinds of entrepreneurs:

1. *Resource Entrepreneurs:* They would focus on the economic realization of the natural, traditional and human resources with the help of customized technology and modern management to enhance the income level of every household. They would perform the critical role of moving resources up the value chain through the application of

best practices and matching product to market. Their performance would be reflected in the overall growth of the GDP of the rural complex.

2. *Social Entrepreneurs:* The other category, the social entrepreneurs, would work closely with the resource entrepreneurs. They would focus on improving the human development index in terms of education, health care and so on. These entrepreneurs would thus promote the conversion of the increased purchasing power into a better life. Their performance would be objectively reflected in the enhanced literacy levels, reduced infant or maternal mortality rate, enhanced nutrition, and access to good habitation, sanitation, clean drinking water and quality energy. They would also lead to environmental consciousness and reduction in societal conflicts.

The entrepreneurs of PURA Activated would work closely with local PURA champions, who may be institutions or organizations of repute. They would be partners of the government, local administration and panchayati raj institutions. The enterprise network of PURA Activated would have to be evolved through technical collaboration with a multidimensional array of technological and managerial institutions. Similarly, enterprises from different parts of the world could be partners of PURA Activated by acting as equity investors, exploring and facilitating market linkages and providing a technological platform for best practices and innovative solutions to production challenges. In this way, enterprises, academic institutions and business units from across the world could share their core competencies to harness the resources of untapped rural and suburban regions and also lead to human development.

USER COMMUNITY PYRAMID

Due to the dwindling of natural resources and burgeoning of population, today it is essential to think of sustainable development in every aspect of human life in every sector of the economy. What is the unique approach that would help us achieve sustainable development? I would like to propose an integrated solution for sustainable development through a unique model called User Community Pyramid (UCP).

UCP is a structure linking the following:

1. Natural Resources

Natural resources are the basis for sustainable development. We have been using natural resources for human development using science and technology and their applications. But, at the same time, we have been polluting the environment in the form of greenhouse gas emission, deforestation and pollution of land, water and air. Today, natural resources are dwindling and the environment is polluted, leading to global warming.

2. Information and Communication

This includes information collection, generation and dissemination through communication networks. It would help monitor and track natural resources and plan for improving the environment. Modern geo-spatial analytical tools would enrich our knowledge about how to bring sustainable development in multiple areas such as waste, pollution, energy, mobility and biodiversity.

3. Convergence of Technologies

Rapid advancements in technology have resulted in many new products and systems in the management of water, energy, environment, pollution, waste, biodiversity and health care. For example, solar technologies have resulted in the first 700 MW solar park in Gujarat; the nano-filter technology has resulted in safe drinking water solutions; and nano-packaging technologies have led to biodegradable packaging solutions. The convergence of these and information and communication technologies is necessary for the progress of humanity.

4. Societal Business Model

On the one hand is the development of technology-based systems through scientific research, while on the other is the evolution of an innovative business model which will take the technologies to the end users. This will empower and enrich farmers, fishermen, skilled workers and people living in the rural areas.

5. Bottom of the Pyramid

The users are the bottom of the pyramid in the UCP. They are
the vital links for all economic activities and the beneficiaries
of sustainable development. Ultimately, all the work has to
benefit them. The technologies have to help improve their
quality of life using the existing natural resources sustainably
for generations to come.

SOCIETAL DEVELOPMENT RADAR

The purpose of establishing a developmental radar is to review
and monitor how the UCP has benefited the users. This would
be based on nine essential empowerment attributes which are
critical to the realization of our goal of a happy, prosperous
and peaceful society. These traits are:
1. Food and nutrition
2. Access to water, both potable and irrigation
3. Access to health care
4. Access to income generation capacity
5. Access to education and capacity building
6. Access to quality power and communication applications
7. State of societal conflict
8. Access to financial services
9. Access to clean and green environment.

There would be three targets for the societal development
radar. One would be the current status of the nine social

attributes. The second would be a medium-term target, followed by the third, a long-term target with a specific schedule.

The concept of PURA, when implemented in this manner, will be a sustainable development system that will uplift the 3 billion rural population of the planet and create an equal and happy world that will be truly great in every respect.

SIXTEEN

CONCLUSION

FRIENDS, IN THE Preface to this book, I recounted my encounter with a foreign tourist on a flight from Bhubaneswar to Delhi and what it indicated to me about our national character. I would like to conclude the book with a similar anecdote.

On the night of 29 November 2011, I was returning from Seoul to Delhi on a non-stop flight after attending a meeting of the Eminent Persons Group. It was organized by the President of South Korea prior to the Seoul Nuclear Security Summit that was to be held the following year. This meet was attended by top experts in the nuclear field from different countries. The mission of the Eminent Persons Group is to establish safety and security guidelines for 539 nuclear power plants spread all over the world. I am not going to talk about the details of that meet, but I would like to share one incident which was narrated by Shinichi Kitaoka, a Japanese political scientist, historian and former diplomat, to me and the other members of the Eminent Persons Group.

The professor was talking about the Fukushima Daiichi nuclear disaster, which had taken place in his homeland in March that year. The energy accident at the Fukushima-I nuclear power plant was initiated by a tsunami following the Tohoku earthquake on 11 March 2011. Immediately after the earthquake, the active reactors automatically shut down their sustained fission reactions. But the tsunami destroyed the emergency generators cooling the reactors, leading to three nuclear meltdowns and the release of radioactive material. Several hydrogen-air chemical explosions occurred over the next few days.

The Fukushima accident was the worst nuclear disaster the world had witnessed since the one at Chernobyl in 1986 in what was then the Soviet Union. But, unlike Chernobyl, there wasn't a single radiation-induced casualty in Fukushima.

'Two Japanese cities were attacked with nuclear weapons in 1945,' Prof. Kitaoka said. 'It was a painful tragedy, but one that Japanese citizens withstood boldly and, within three decades, Japan was transformed into one of the most industrialized nations in the world. Now, the Fukushima nuclear power plant problem is in front of us. We the Japanese will not allow this problem to become our master. With international cooperation, we the Japanese will become the master of the problem, defeat the problem and succeed, and the world will see clean and green nuclear energy flourishing all around.'

A great nation is one which, when faced with a grave

challenge, rises to the occasion and brings out the best in itself. The people of the nation work as one to become the master of the problem and defeat it. That is the national character of a great country like Japan.

India has a lot to learn from the examples of such great nations. When I visit different panchayats, villages and municipal corporations in India, I am able to assess within an hour or two of my visit whether the place is properly administered by good leaders. I am also able to judge whether the citizens of the area work as one in taking responsibility for their homes, neighbourhood, village or city. Unfortunately, more often than not, I find this spirit lacking in the lay citizens as well as their elected representatives at every level of government.

This trend must change if India is to occupy the pride of place that rightfully belongs to her in the world order. It is our collective responsibility. I sincerely hope that this book, particularly the oaths drafted for different groups of people from all walks of life, helps India's citizenry rise to this great responsibility and develop a national character that enables our nation to lead the whole world on the pathways to greatness.

INDEX

Index

User Community Pyramid
(UCP), 146, 148

Vajpayee, Atal Behari, 116–17,
119
Venkataraman, R., 102
Vidyasagar, M., 103
Vishnu Narayan, Pandit, 129
Vivekananda, Swami, 62

waste management, closed loop
system, 19–21

Wayanad, Kerala, 28–30
World Toilet Organization, 13
human genome project, 3–4,
112

Yoga Sutra (Patanjali), 108

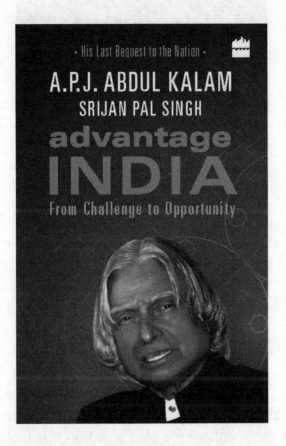

Dr Kalam, writing with Srijan Pal Singh, shows how it can be 'Advantage India' in the final lap of the journey to 2020 – the landmark year by which he had envisioned the country could transform into an economic power.

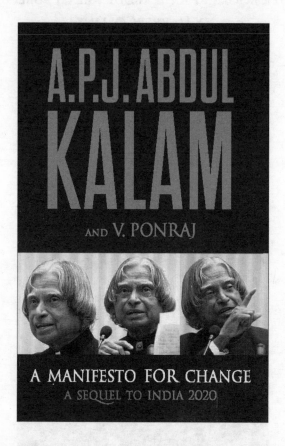

A.P.J. ABDUL KALAM

AND V. PONRAJ

A MANIFESTO FOR CHANGE
A SEQUEL TO INDIA 2020

In this sequel to *India 2020*, Dr Kalam, writing with V. Ponraj, draws up a plan of action that looks at development from the grassroots so that India can take giant strides in all walks of life and accomplish the goal of becoming a developed nation.

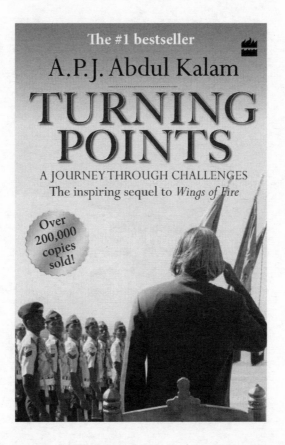

The #1 bestseller

A.P.J. Abdul Kalam

TURNING POINTS

A JOURNEY THROUGH CHALLENGES

The inspiring sequel to *Wings of Fire*

Over 200,000 copies sold!

Perennially on bestseller charts since it was first published in 2012, *Turning Points* takes up the incredible Kalam story from where *Wings of Fire* left off. It brings together little-known details from his career and presidency as he speaks out on points of controversy.

HarperCollins*Publishers*India

🐦 @HarperCollinsIN

📷 @HarperCollinsIN

📘 @HarperCollinsIN

💼 HarperCollins Publishers India

www.harpercollins.co.in

Harper Broadcast

Showcasing celebrated authors, book reviews, plot trailers, cover reveals, launches and interviews, Harper Broadcast is live and available for free subscription on the brand's social media channels through a new newsletter. Hosted by renowned TV anchor and author Amrita Tripathi, Broadcast is a snapshot of all that is news, views, extracts, sneak peeks and opinions on books. Tune in to conversations with authors, where we get up close and personal about their books, why they write and what's coming up.

Harper Broadcast is the first of its kind in India, a publisher-hosted news channel for all things publishing within HarperCollins. Follow us on Twitter and YouTube.

Subscribe to the monthly newsletter here: https://harpercollins.co.in/newsletter/

📺 Harper Broadcast

🐦 @harperbroadcast

www.harperbroadcast.com

Address

HarperCollins Publishers India Ltd
A-75, Sector 57, Noida, UP 201301, India

Phone
+91-120-4044800

25 ⬛ HarperCollins India Ltd

Celebrating 25 Years of Great Publishing

HarperCollins India celebrates its twenty-fifth anniversary in 2017. Twenty-five years of publishing India's finest writers and some of its most memorable books – those you cannot put down; ones you want to finish reading yet don't want to end; works you can read over and over again only to fall deeper in love with.

Through the years, we have published writers from the Indian subcontinent, and across the globe, including Aravind Adiga, Kiran Nagarkar, Amitav Ghosh, Jhumpa Lahiri, Manu Joseph, Anuja Chauhan, Upamanyu Chatterjee, A.P.J. Abdul Kalam, Shekhar Gupta, M.J. Akbar, Satyajit Ray, Gulzar, Surender Mohan Pathak and Anita Nair, amongst others, with approximately 200 new books every year and an active print and digital catalogue of more than 1,000 titles, across ten imprints. Publishing works of various genres including literary fiction, poetry, mind body spirit, commercial fiction, journalism, business, self-help, cinema, biographies – all with attention to quality, of the manuscript and the finished product – it comes as no surprise that we have won every major literary award including the Man Booker Prize, the Sahitya Akademi Award, the DSC Prize, the Hindu Literary Prize, the MAMI Award for Best Writing on Cinema, the National Award for Best Book on Cinema, the Crossword Book Award, and the Publisher of the Year, twice, at Publishing Next in Goa and, in 2016, at Tata Literature Live, Mumbai.

We credit our success to the people who make us who we are, and will be celebrating this anniversary with: our authors, retailers, partners, readers and colleagues at HarperCollins India. Over the years, a firm belief in our promise and our passion to deliver only the very best of the printed word has helped us become one of India's finest in publishing. Every day we endeavour to deliver bigger and better – for you.

Thank you for your continued support and patronage.